Coaching Educational Leadership

BELMAS

British Educational Leadership, Management & Administration Society

Published in association with the British Educational Leadership, Management and Administration Society.

This series of books published for BELMAS aims to be directly relevant to the concerns and professional development needs of emergent leaders and experienced leaders in schools.

Titles include:

Managing Special and Inclusive Education
By Steve Rayner (2007)

How Very Effective Primary Schools Work (2006)
By Chris James, Michael Connolly and Gerald Dunning

Educational Leadership: Personal Growth for Professional Development (2004)
By Harry Tomlinson

Developing Educational Leadership: Using Evidence for Policy and Practice (2003)
By Lesley Anderson and Nigel Bennett

Performance Management in Education: Improving Practice (2002)
By Jenny Reeves, Pauline Smith, Harry Tomlinson and Christine Ford

Strategic Management for School Development: Leading Your School's Improvement Strategy (2002)
By Brian Fidler

Subject Leadership and School Improvement (2000)
By Hugh Busher and Alma Harris with Christine Wise

Coaching Educational Leadership

Building Leadership Capacity through Partnership

JAN ROBERTSON

$SAGE

Los Angeles | London | New Delhi
Singapore | Washington DC

First published in 2005 by NZCER PRESS, The New Zealand Council for Educational Research, PO Box 3237, Wellington, New Zealand. © Jan Robertson 2005. Reprinted 2006.

This edition published 2008 under license from NZCER.

Reprinted 2009

SAGE Publications Ltd
1 Oliver's Yard
55 City Road
London EC1Y 1SP

SAGE Publications Inc.
2455 Teller Road
Thousand Oaks, California 91320

SAGE Publications India Pvt Ltd
B 1/I 1 Mohan Cooperative Industrial Area
Mathura Road
New Delhi 110 044

SAGE Publications Asia-Pacific Pte Ltd
33 Pekin Street #02-01
Far East Square
Singapore 048763

Library of Congress Control Number: 2007939520

British Library Cataloguing in Publication data

A catalogue record for this book is available from the British Library

ISBN 978-1-84787-403-0
ISBN 978-1-84787-404-7 (pbk)

Typeset by C&M Digitals (P) Ltd., Chennai, India
Printed in Great Britain by CPI Antony Rowe, Chippenham, Wiltshire
Printed on paper from sustainable resources

FSC
Mixed Sources
Product group from well-managed forests and other controlled sources
Cert no. SGS-COC-2953
www.fsc.org
© 1996 Forest Stewardship Council

To my daughter, my sister and my mother—my coaches,
my heroes, my friends.

"An accessible read with insights for all leaders who want to continue to grow professionally."

Lorna M. Earl, PhD, Aporia Consulting

"This is a welcome and timely contribution for leaders everywhere."

Louise Stoll, Visiting Professor, Institute of Education, University of London

"Your leadership [coaching] programme has firstly had me reflect on my current beliefs and practice, then challenge me through research and debate to develop further as a leader ... The whole process has got me away from an emphasis on management and a far better appreciation of the potential growth influence I can generate from being the school's educational leader. Thank you."

Garry De Thierry, Principal, Rotorua Intermediate School, New Zealand

Contents

A FINAL NOTE

Foreword

Whenever I have to arrange an appointment with an educational leader I am meeting for the first time, the leader will typically caution me that he or she is very busy and can only spare a few minutes; that there isn't much time. The recurring and paradoxical experience is that once through the door of the leader's office, I then find myself trapped, a captive audience, unable to escape. Over the course of an hour, an hour-and-a-half, or more, leader after leader insists on regaling me with stories of their achievements and setbacks, their hopes and plans for the future, their reminiscences and regrets about the past, their long lists of frustrations with the system, and their poignant portrayals of breakthroughs with the students and adults who matter to them most.

Sometimes, after an age of agonizing and complaining about the frustrations of the job – the overwork, the bureaucracy, the lack of appreciation, the imperious superiors with their unreasonable demands, and the "blockers" in their staff who repeatedly sabotage their best efforts – I will then ask the leader I am with whether, if given the chance, they would choose to lead all over again. The response is almost always immediate and emphatic – "Oh yes. It's wonderful work. I wouldn't dream of doing anything else!"

Educational leadership is one of the most rewarding and also frustrating jobs there is. The rewards keep leaders going. The frustrations drive them out. What typically tips the balance is whether educational leaders face the challenges together or alone.

Leaders are surrounded by other adults and in the best communities, they can face the challenges of change together, as colleagues, almost as equals. But even here, so many of the most difficult problems, worries, and doubts in leadership are hard to share with or disclose to those leaders whom you are charged to lead. You can't vent your frustration about "resisters" or "blockers" without descending into tittle-tattle and gossip. You can't air your uncertainties about your next career step, or about who might succeed you, without spreading anxiety throughout your community. And sometimes, in the darkest moments that afflict all leaders, when you doubt your very capacity to lead, it's hard to imagine, outside your own family, anyone with whom you can share any of these feelings at all.

If leadership has always been lonely work, it is becoming lonelier still. The administration who were once teachers' colleagues have now been forcibly separated by many governments into separate unions and associations, and converted into supervisors and managers as a result. Economic cutbacks and moves towards site-based management have removed the layer of support and mentoring that many educational leaders were once able to turn to. My own research on educational change over thirty years in eight Canadian and US high schools reveals that whereas leaders were once seen as being larger than life characters who were visibly attached to their schools, that they made their mark upon, and stayed in for a long time, school leaders now are seen as being interchangeable managers who turn over regularly and serve the government or themselves rather than the schools in which they work (Hargreaves & Fink, 2005).

In my own school improvement work, one of the greatest benefits repeatedly cited by leaders is the opportunity that has been created for them to meet once a month with their colleagues and discuss openly, without fear and in an environment of complete trust, their recent achievements, their difficulties in dealing with imposed reform agendas, and their responses to research findings that cast light upon their work. These peer support groups of committed and concerned colleagues are invaluable assets to leadership development and retention. They keep leaders going.

In addition to their form of group support, my colleague Irwin Blumer advises that all school or school system leaders should be provided with a mentor and a coach. The mentor knows your school and its people. The coach is not swayed by their knowledge and experience of the individuals concerned, but understands the job and how people experience it.

This book, by Jan Robertson, is the first of its kind to deal with the theory and practice of leadership coaching. Drawing on years of researching leadership as well as leading herself, Robertson draws on an impressive range of theory and research in psychology, sociology, business management, and organizational development to get to grips with the essence of coaching, the benefits it can provide, and the difficulties of conducting it. Using her extensive contact with leaders and leadership around the world, Robertson puts the theory to work in real life examples of leaders coaching leaders–elucidating how professional development, career development, leaders' motivation, lifelong learning, and organizational improvement all benefit as a result.

Robertson is a realist. Neither a Pollyanna professor nor a critical prophet of doom, Robertson deals with leadership and leadership coaching as it is, bringing it to life in ways that will give hope to and also make sense to all these leaders who read her work. Practical strategies and guided reflection take the coaches and the coached far beyond the old rudiments of clinical supervision into the complexities and possibilities of leadership coaching today–embedded in rather than separate from organizational improvement and professional development.

Whatever our work, all of us can benefit from the perspective of a critical friend, a coach and advocate, who stands by our side, gives us pause to reflect, and helps us to eventually move forward. Even nine-year-old soccer players get a coach. It's time that all our educational leaders on the front line are provided with one as well. Jan Robertson's splendid book not only advocates articulately for the necessity of leadership coaching, but sets out practically what really good coaching can and should look like.

Andy Hargreaves
Boston College

References

Hargreaves, A. & Fink, D. (2005) *Sustainable Leadership.* San Francisco, CA: Jossey-Bass/Wiley.

Preface

This book is about coaching leadership, and it has been written for anyone who is interested and involved in improving educational leadership and learning—their own and others. Although my focus is the field of education, the principles and practices outlined can be, and have been, used effectively in other contexts, such as learning organisations in the corporate world.

Coaching Educational Leadership will assist individual leaders[1] wanting to reflect on their own leadership, the adviser working with educational leaders in the field, educational leaders in an institution who are responsible for leading others and for developing teaching and learning, and classroom teachers wanting to reflect more effectively on the way they facilitate learning. It can help boards of trustee members and other leaders conduct appraisal more effectively, and challenge those involved in the professional development of educational leaders to critique their programmes and the way they work. Most importantly, it will assist those leaders who are interested in establishing coaching relationships for leadership development.

Although there are many "how to" coaching books on the market, this book highlights, and builds on, 15 years of research and development in the field of leadership coaching. I first took up academic research when I was in a principalship. The work I did was on effective schools. It whetted my appetite and led me to ask why I had not previously been acquainted with all this theory and research. During my career I have held many leadership roles in education—senior teacher, principal, assistant dean, head of department, director—and within each there was little specific leadership development, formal professional feedback or critique of my practice available. These experiences and roles taught me much about leadership and allowed me to work with leaders of incredible talent, but I became concerned, and particularly so at the time of my principalship, at the lack of specific job-related professional opportunities for leadership development. The dearth

---

1. The use of the word "leaders", rather than designated positions such as teacher, principal, head of department, lecturer, or CEO, in this book is deliberate. This book is about coaching leadership development and so focuses on the leadership responsibilities that all those in education should take up, whatever their position in the institution may be.

of professional dialogue, particularly within the rural principals' group, alarmed me even more. Sports' days, busing issues and other organisational and managerial issues always took precedence over any discussion and debate on leading learning in the school and community. When I moved into the higher education environment in 1989, my study of and research about leadership development began in earnest.

Developing ideas

At this time, both nationally and internationally, there was little national policy relating to, or interest about, educational leadership and its development. With New Zealand's educational institutions moving into self-management as a result of changes in educational policy at the end of the 1980s and beginning of the 1990s, the impetus for management development increased. The government provided one year of professional development support to school principals and their boards, but after the first year of the reforms, individual institutions were generally left to look for leadership support and development from other sources. Much of the rhetoric at the time was managerial and isolated principals from their teaching profession, but, paradoxically, what they needed to *be* self-managing was a greater focus on educational leadership and the ability to build social and intellectual capacity in their institutions.

This paradox created dilemmas for those in education management positions (Robertson, 1991a). Many failed to adapt to the new roles, responsibilities, and tensions, and left the profession. Some struggled and found ways of working within the new political context. Others were ready to try new ways of working that took up the intellectual independence offered through self-management, while finding ways to resist, contest or hijack the managerialist ideology that abounded (Strachan, 1999). It was evident that a new type of professional development was necessary for leaders in the new self-managing institutions.

The work of Hallinger and Murphy (1985, 1991) on principalship at this time, along with later work on problem-based learning (Hallinger & Bridges, 1997), influenced my belief in the importance of developing an authentic model of leadership development, especially for use in university-based programmes. This belief led to the establishment of the first Educational *Leadership* Centre in New Zealand in 1990 at the University of Waikato, when elsewhere the focus was on establishing and maintaining centres for *principals* and developing educational administration and management qualifications rather than leadership qualifications.

Debate also arose around this time as to whether leadership is a discipline in its own right, and it was with this debate in mind that I accepted a Fulbright Scholarship in 1992. The scholarship took me to Vanderbilt University in Tennessee, the Far West Laboratory in San Francisco, the Harvard Principals' Center in Boston, the Washington, DC Educational Leadership Center, and many other places where leadership development was both exciting and challenging. The Danforth Foundation was very influential in the USA at this time, impacting on at least 22 university programmes by 1992. Its work focused specifically on "changing the way we prepare educational leaders" (to use the title of a book by Milstein & Associates, 1993), with the aim of making programmes for the study of school leadership more relevant and contextually specific. My motivation for, and commitment to, centring my career on educational leadership development in New Zealand were cemented and ensured.

At this time, too, scholars around the world were interested in New Zealand's full-scale move to site-based administration of education institutions. I was invited to speak at an international conference in Thailand, at Chiang Mai University's Center for Leadership Research and Development, and, later, at other international conferences exploring decentralisation, in Canada, Singapore, Australia, Malaysia, and the USA. These engagements allowed me to exchange ideas on leadership development with international colleagues working in this exciting field. Today, there are many strong international networks of scholars working, increasingly collaboratively, to develop the field of educational leadership.

This book encapsulates the ideas drawn from dialogue over many years among numerous educational leaders about professional development through coaching. The empirical data presented in these pages are drawn from my study of leaders coaching each other over a three-year period and my ongoing research and development programmes in this area. These data, the collection of which has been informed by the aforementioned ideas, form the basis of the model of leadership coaching documented in this book. My use of the theory and practice of action research throughout the model's development makes the model a continually developing entity. Many graduate students, all successful leaders themselves in education, health and business, have studied, researched and practised this model, and developed it further in a variety of contexts in the public and private sectors (see, for example, Sutton, 2005).

The coaching model has been used by teams in early childhood centres, with curriculum development and classroom management in mathematics in secondary schools (Winters, 1996), in higher education departments in New Zealand and Thailand and with teacher education advisers in Indonesia (Fadillah, 1997), and with teacher appraisal in higher education in the Solomon Islands (Houma, 1998). It has also been used in various national development contracts, in Information Communication Technology (ICT) development with secondary leaders in Hong Kong (SAR) (T. Lee, 2002), with groups of school leaders in England and Australia, and with over 300 school leaders in Singapore. In short, the model has been continually and consistently developed and researched, across education contexts and cultures, over the last decade.

This sustained engagement with others studying the professional development of educational leaders, the many addresses, workshops, and dialogic encounters, both national and international, have all in some way informed the model and, therefore, this book. I would therefore like to thank people who have helped me to get it written. Lorna Earl, Louise Stoll, Alma Harris, and Andy Hargreaves provided continued professional and personal support and encouragement, and commentary on developing ideas. Pare Kana taught me the lived meanings of *ako* and *aroha* and their importance in coaching. It is an honour to be able to include cartoons by Donn Ratana, the resident artist at the University of Waikato. Mike Milstein warrants special thanks for his extensive feedback on the developing manuscript, as does Bev Webber, Publishing Manager of NZCER, for believing in the idea I had for this book, and giving critical, insightful feedback at key stages in the process. I sincerely thank Paula Wagemaker for so skilfully editing the final manuscript. A special thanks too, to Marianne Lagrange for bringing this book to the international audience. I must thank, too, the many educational leaders I have worked with in New Zealand, England, Canada and elsewhere overseas who have assisted in critiquing and developing the coaching model. I pay special tribute to Ginny Lee and Bruce Barnett for their work in peer-assisted leadership development and interest in my work in the early years, and also to Jane Strachan, a friend, professional colleague and "coach" in my own leadership journey as we worked together, using the skills presented in this book. Yvette Shore has also worked with me on the developing ideas since the inception of the Leadership Centre, and her encouragement and creativity have been immeasurable. Finally, I want to thank my family for the love they give me in life. This book would not have been written without their ongoing support.

I have found my journey stimulating and challenging, and I hope that as you read this book you will become as committed as I am to a model of developing leadership through professional coaching. I believe that coaching is the main route to distributed, capacity-building leadership within any institution, and that it facilitates the development of a particular type of educational culture, one that is not only pervasive but also invitational (Stoll & Fink, 1996)—to innovation, to learning, to leadership sustainability (Fullan, 2005; Hargreaves, 2004; Hargreaves & Fink, 2004) and to continual renewal.

The structure of the book

This book is structured to assist you to understand leadership coaching. It has two main parts, followed by a concluding section framed as a "final note". Part One, "Theory", outlines the conceptual framework of the coaching model—the principles, the pedagogy, the methodology, and the research. "Practice" (Part Two) gives detailed examples of how to develop the skills and facilitate the process of coaching. It also identifies the challenges you need to consider during and beyond coaching. Ongoing critical reflection about leadership and its development is vital.

Part One: Theory

The first chapter of this section introduces coaching, providing a definition of it and the principles behind the model. It establishes the rationale for coaching and outlines the research and development that informs the model. Chapter 2 defines and emphasises the importance of *educational* leadership. It describes why coaching practices build leadership capacity and how leaders then become leaders of leaders. It looks at the reality of leaders' work, which, rather than being inimical to coaching occurring, can be the very reason why coaching is so necessary.

Chapter 3 outlines research and theory on effective lifelong learning and professional development. It looks particularly at how coaching crosses the borders between theory and practice, and between professional leadership contexts, to provide authentic, vicarious learning situations. The fourth chapter presents the research findings from empirical studies on the model of leadership coaching presented in this book.

Chapter 5 explores the theory behind action research and demonstrates how leadership coaching can lead to action research and establish a community of learners within and between institutions. It presents an action research case study of how a principal worked to develop a shared vision in her education community.

Part Two: Practice

The first chapter of this section (Chapter 6) outlines how to select a partner, how to get coaching started, and how to develop coaching relationships. It sets out a typical coaching session and a year's coaching programme. It also presents some key ideas from a case study of two leaders getting started in their partnership and demonstrates how the coaching relationship develops over time. Chapter 7 describes the skills of listening, reflective interviewing, and context interviewing, all necessary for developing coaching as a professional development practice and for establishing trust and understanding.

The continuing development of skills in the coaching process is set out in Chapter 8. Self-assessment, goal setting, observing, and describing practice, giving evaluative feedback and knowledge of the change process are outlined. In Chapter 9, we look at what happens when things do not go as smoothly as hoped. The focus here is on troubleshooting within coaching and exploring what leads to the success or failure of the developing relationships. This chapter also looks at the importance of continuously evaluating and carrying out meta-reflections of coaching practices; some reflective exercises are given for coaching partners to use for this purpose.

Chapter 10 gives guidance on facilitating the process of coaching and the roles of the coach when establishing coaching relationships with and between leaders. The three case studies in Chapter 11 show first how leaders become qualified coaches through completing the year-long coaching programme and then how they can use the coaching model within their own institutions and professional organisations. Chapter 12 explores the development of agency and self-efficacy through leadership coaching. The case study presented in this chapter reveals how the experience of coaching gave a leader enough support and encouragement to deal with a leadership issue with the Education Review Office in New Zealand.

"A Final Note", the concluding section of the book, is subtitled "Beyond Coaching? Breaking the Boundaries". While acting as a conclusion to the book, this section also posits where to go from here and stresses the importance of developing capable leaders, and leadership capacity in ourselves and in our institutions. It looks at the research on boundary-breaking leadership development and learning and considers how the principles of coaching, learning communities, and boundary-breaking leadership link together. Thinking about how coaching can be used as an agent of change and transformation within wider society is the final challenge put to readers.

A little more explanation

Direct quotations from leaders who participated in the research studies are highlighted throughout the book. These not only capture and portray the richness of these leaders' experiences, their frustrations, and their leadership learning along the way, but also remind you that the ideas in this book are based on empirical research. The case studies in four of the chapters describe how different leaders worked together, their leadership actions, and their subsequent critical reflection on those actions. They demonstrate how these people developed the conviction that they were educational leaders who could act in an alternative, transformative manner, and who, through this new learning, could make a positive difference in education. The activities included in some of the "Practice" chapters challenge you to reflect critically on leadership. Coaching facilitators (i.e., people who facilitate the coaching practice of others) can also use them to develop the coaching skills of those with whom they are working.

The chapters are basically chronological in that they detail the evolving nature of the action research studies and the thinking behind the development of the model. I must emphasise here that the book does not signal the culmination of this thinking, but rather, within the framework of "grounded theory", is always only the beginning—never the final word:

> The sociological perspective is never finished, not even when the last line of the monograph is written. Not even after it has been published, since therefore the researchers find themselves elaborating and amending their theory, knowing more now than when the research was formally concluded. (Glaser & Strauss, 1967, p. 256)

I consider that my learning in this area will never be complete, and so ideas will continue to develop. As the chapters show, the learning I have gained from how other leaders have applied this model in the field (for some examples, see Chapter 11) has helped me refine it, critique it and develop it in new ways. As the chapters also show, the leaders I have worked with developed their coaching partnerships uniquely, but had the shared experience of working in critically reflective ways with their colleagues. Their comments (and those of other leaders who have engaged with the model) at the end of their coaching experiences highlight the fulfilment that the more formal professional interaction achieved through the coaching model brought them. The following comments are typical:

> This has been one of the most—no, *the* most!—professionally supportive experiences of my 39 years in the job!

> I hope we keep up this coaching partnership. It is my best development undertaken! Even my staff comment on this.

> We feel we have gained substantially.

I hope your experiences will be equally positive as you develop and practise the skills of coaching with a professional partner (and preferably with some external assistance with this process). I also hope that, after you have embedded the coaching experiences into your own practice, you will begin to work with others to develop the practices and principles of learning by exercising coaching in your and their institutions.

Jan Robertson

PART ONE:
THEORY

Introduction

CHAPTER OVERVIEW

This chapter begins by defining leadership coaching as presented in this book. It outlines the reasons why this form of coaching is essential in the current education context, and from there moves to an overview of various international leadership development ideas and theories. The chapter then traces the empirical research underpinning the development of the coaching model documented in this book and the key principles and ideas upon which it is based. The chapter concludes by describing the three research studies that produced the model.

What is coaching and why coaching?

Coaching defined

Coaching, as presented in this book, is a special, sometimes reciprocal, relationship between (at least) two people who work together to set professional goals *and* achieve them. The term depicts a learning relationship, where participants are open to new learning, engage together as professionals equally committed to facilitating each other's leadership learning development and wellbeing (both cognitive and affective), and gain a greater understanding of professionalism and the work of professionals.

Dialogue is the essence of coaching and the concurrent improvement of practice. Leaders elect to be coached because they want to improve their practice on an ongoing basis. The coaching model in this book assumes that two leaders believe they will gain equal, but different, benefits from working with each other as they develop and implement their professional and personal goals.

Underlying premises

Several premises inform the definition of coaching. The first is that educational leaders are often teachers by preparation, and so effective leadership development should include many of the principles that underpin effective teacher development.

The second is that professional development should be a lifelong process. Although leaders may be at different stages of their careers, all need ongoing opportunities to renew, refresh, and redirect their educational leadership practice. New expectations and roles necessitate this—the only constant in education, after all, is change. There will always be a need for leaders to change direction—to branch out into new areas of development. New leaders, moreover, need to be able to embrace change for the possibilities and opportunities it can bring. All leaders have the responsibility to keep on learning throughout their career.

The third premise is that people who are influential in education should focus, as their main priority, on educational leadership that improves learning. Thrupp and Willmott (2003) describe this focus as "critical leadership", where there is not only reflection on learning but also a "public commitment to doing things differently" (p. 180) and "reflection on wider issues of social structure and politics" (p. 181). This stance requires continual critique of the role and practice of leadership in learning and articulation of the dilemmas and tensions faced within that context.

A fourth premise is that linking theory and research to the study of issues relating to the first three premises and their leadership practices is the key to successful leadership development. That is why coaching provided by practitioners and academic specialists working in partnership can be very effective. The coaching peers provide each other with professional feedback and vicarious learning through the observation necessary for leadership development. The academic professional provides the coaching partners with challenges, critical perspectives, skills, and theories that support and challenge their developing coaching practices. There must be challenge if the professional relationship that coaching partners develop is to serve an educative purpose. The partners also need to be supported and encouraged for changes in behaviour to occur. Outside perspectives are thus paramount in bringing effective change to leaders' practice. This facilitative role is explored in greater depth in Chapter 10.

New leaders for new times

Today, there is increased interest internationally in leadership develop-ment and coaching, and this area is now hailed as worthy of renewed respect. This interest has had particular resonance in New Zealand, where the changes brought about by policy developments in the late 1980s and early 1990s led to a focus on self-management of educational institutions and brought particular challenges for leadership. The time was right to begin to explore the use of a coaching model for the development and support of such leadership.

New Zealand was the first (and perhaps sole) country in the world to move to full-scale decentralisation of educational provision across all sectors. The advent of self-management in New Zealand required a new type of leader, and new ways of developing the skills he or she would need. More specifically, the country needed educational leaders who could

- build capacity and commitment;
- build strong relationships and partnerships;
- focus on learning;

- understand the change process; and
- see the importance of finding new approaches to "doing" and "being".

As Caldwell (2002, p. 843) has observed, the need since that time has been for "new approaches to professionalism [that] will challenge the modest levels of knowledge and skill that sufficed in the past, with a vision for values-centred, outcomes-oriented, data-driven and team-focused approaches that matches or even exceeds that of the best of medical practice." For Gronn (2002), "designer leadership development" (his term) based on competencies and standards will not create the types of leaders needed today, for much the same reason articulated by Lupton (2004, p. 31), who contends that "the wide variation between [institutions] ... may give rise for differentiated strategies" rather than a one-size-fits-all approach effected through the development of leadership competencies devoid of context. Because the context in which leadership operates markedly influences how that leadership is exercised, development and support initiatives need to focus on the local context—nationally, regionally, and institutionally. This is not always the case in leadership development initiatives around the world.

The need for relevance and challenge

> "That is the beauty of this programme. We can relate what we are thinking and feeling and doing, to what we are feeling at the time, not to some academic or theoretical thing that we think might happen—it is happening and we talk about it."

Essentially, if we are to acknowledge the reality and context of leaders' work, then we must establish the type of professional development that will support their daily practice. It is important that leaders can see the direct relevance of their professional development to practice. Development activities far removed from the reality of their work serve no purpose. Educational leaders need to be working with the people, issues, and concerns they face daily if they are to see the need for, and relevance of, leadership development.

Often missing from the theory on effective professional development is *how* leaders can put professional development in place that contains all the principles identified as important. How do we get those in education to see that change and development in their leadership behaviour are necessary and important? The answer is, as the above definition of coaching implies, challenge. Leaders must be challenged to understand and reflect on how changing their practice will make a difference. Peer coaching provides that challenge, and even more so when coaching partners share their perspectives with other such partnerships in learning communities. The variety of perspectives, the development of activities and skills, and the presence of support all serve as professional development opportunities that enhance coaching relationships.

The leadership development context today

Reconceptualisations

Among the governments worldwide that are moving forward with national policy for leadership development, England's has taken a particularly strong lead in recent years with the establishment of the country's National College for School Leadership. A key focus of the National College is learning-centred leadership and personalised development (Southworth, 2002). A recent study of 15 countries shows many mandatory or quasi-mandatory programmes throughout Europe, Asia, Australasia, and North America (Huber, 2003).

These programmes represent a giant step forward from the early 1990s when interest in school leadership preparation and development was of "relatively little interest" outside the USA (Hallinger, 2003). The programmes also show major paradigm shifts in leadership development, particularly over the last decade. Initiatives have moved a long way from the early days of clinical supervision models (Goldhammer, 1969; Joyce & Showers, 1982), but certain elements and key principles of these have survived the test of time (Joyce & Showers, 1988). Although some policy makers still tend to favour "informed prescription" of leadership development curricula (Barber, 2002), the education profession now places greater emphasis on initiatives such as learning communities (Stoll & Bolam, 2005), coaching and mentoring (e.g., Singapore Educational Administration Society), peer-assisted leadership (PAL), leadership centres, problem-based learning (Hallinger & Bridges, 1997), and action-research communities. These initiatives all focus on building leadership capacity in individuals and in institutions (Harris & Lambert, 2003), distributed leadership (Gronn, 2003; Harris, 2004), and "data-literate" and evidence-based leadership (Earl & Katz, 2002; Southworth, 2002). In so doing, they have enhanced belief in "informed professional judgement" (Barber, 2002). Various commentators, A. Hargreaves (2003) and D. Hargreaves (2003) among them, stress that networks advantage teacher, institutional, and systemic change.

A number of associations and journals focus solely on school effectiveness and improvement. One such professional association is the International Congress for School Effectiveness and Improvement, with its flagship journal, *School Effectiveness and School Improvement* (SESI). Some of these associations have added "leadership" to their name to signify a change of emphasis (e.g., BELMAS, which stands for the British Educational Leadership, Management, and Administration Society, and NZEALS—the New Zealand Educational Leadership and Administration Society). Similarly, many academic journals now focus solely on the theory and practice of leadership. Two recent editions of the *International Handbook of Educational Leadership and Administration* (see, for example, Leithwood & Hallinger, 2002) honour and validate leadership thinking from around the world. Such emphases have informed our collective co-construction of knowledge about leadership learning and given us a much better understanding of this area internationally.

The past decade or so has also seen a reconceptualisation of leadership. Sergiovanni (1992) and Fullan (2003a) have advanced our understanding of moral and authentic leadership, while Strachan (1999) and Starratt (2004) have looked respectively at critical leadership for social justice and spirituality in leadership. Gronn (2003) and Thrupp's (2004) call for a move away from "designer models of leadership development" to a more critical focus has been accompanied by calls for cross-cultural and boundary-breaking leadership (Robertson & Webber, 2002; Shields, 2002; Walker & Dimmock, 2002).

Key principles and ideas

Reciprocity, structure, and support

Different coaching models abound, so it is important that the principles underlying the model in this book are reiterated and maintained when developing coaching relationships. The work of Cochran-Smith and Lytle (1993) is reflected in many of the principles, which include or focus on:

- the legitimation and validation of leaders' practice;
- the development of theory by practitioners;
- the informing and changing of leaders' practice;
- the importance of operating at the interface of theory and practice;
- the need to provide support and challenge in leadership development;
- the need to set up a structure that will help leaders continue their development unassisted;
- the development of a model that any leader can use anywhere and in whatever context;
- a belief in "leaders as knowers" rather than "coaches as knowers"—that is, validating leaders as theory makers;
- a belief in leaders as lifelong learners; and
- a desire to alter the traditional relationships between professionals and between institutions.

Several key ideas also inform the model:

1. The process is dynamic, meeting the changing needs of and resulting in new learning for each person. In this way it is also reciprocal.
2. The coach is the facilitator of the learning process, not the "teacher" of how something should or could be done, unless invited.
3. The coached person takes responsibility for his or her own learning, and sets the agenda and goals for the coaching sessions.
4. The partners have a good understanding of each other's role and the social and political context within which they both work.
5. The coaching relationship takes time to develop effectively and sustain, with educational change, innovation and improvement occurring over time.
6. The coaching partners require the interpersonal, communication and coaching skills to work together in different ways.

The role of the coach

Both the person doing the coaching and the person being coached must be taught the skills of coaching and should discuss the principles behind these. When two people know how to play the game, coaching is easy. It is therefore important that the coaches of each partnership empower the coached to make their own decisions about their leadership practice.

> "I believe at least 60 to 70 percent of the value of coaching is the mere fact that two leaders with a lot in common, in terms of both successes and problems, can sit down and share these honestly and openly, and be helpful to each other."

Coaches do not tell leaders who are being coached how they should lead but rather assist them to reflect critically on their practice so they can make informed decisions about their leadership. The responsibility for learning must be left in the hands of each leader. Leaders who have been well coached in how best to work with each other advance their respective professional development and offer supervision and oversight of each other's practice.

Executive coaching, life coaching, and personal coaching—all prevalent in the literature today—are often conducted by coaches with little, if any, experience of working within the context of the person they are coaching. In this book, coaching is seen as a reciprocal process, conducted by partners who are from, or have been from, similar positions or roles, and who are, to all intents, equal in their relationship. Coaching partners bring to the relationship not only knowledge of the context in question and different strengths and wisdom, but also, and more importantly, different perspectives and an outside (albeit perhaps less subjective) view of a leadership situation. The coaching relationship is dynamic and constantly changing to meet the needs of the people involved. And even though a coaching relationship may not be truly reciprocal, it can be bi-directional in that both partners gain in different ways, especially if in different roles, such as leadership coach, education consultant, facilitator or adviser, or principal. Such a relationship can also be effective in terms of critiquing the coaching practice if established on the principles set out in this book.

The development of the coaching model

The model of leadership coaching in this book has evolved over a decade of research and development—some undertaken by me and some by my graduate students. Other research literature has also influenced the model's development in the field. However, the three major pieces of research that had the greatest impact on the developing model are described in the following sections. The model is evolving still, as I participate in critical reflection around the process of coaching, with professional colleagues here and overseas.

The first research study

A naturalistic, qualitative study, involving primary, intermediate, and secondary school leaders during the first year of the Tomorrow School's reforms to education administration in New Zealand (Lange, 1988) was considered an important precursor to understanding the role and needs of these leaders and to identifying the most effective professional development for them during a time of major administrative and curriculum change. I spent one year shadowing 11 leaders from across the school system (primary, intermediate, secondary), in a cluster of schools in an urban city. I interviewed each leader on at least three occasions, organised professional development activities for them, and then evaluated these experiences with them. The aim of this study was to develop some substantive theory about appropriate and effective educational leadership development.

The findings indicated that site-based professional development, which included outside perspectives (i.e., another person's observation and views) on the concerns these leaders were experiencing at that time, was most valuable. This and other related research led me to conclude (Robertson, 1991a, p. 130) that leaders' professional development should:

- acknowledge the realities of their daily practice;
- acknowledge the philosophic, values, and visionary elements in the leaders' work;
- offer opportunities for values development and resolving dilemmas;
- have a strong emphasis on educational leadership;
- encourage critical reflective practice and experiential learning rather than offer *a priori* theoretical or prescribed models;
- be needs based, participatory, and collaborative;
- focus on problem posing as well as problem resolution;
- be developmental over time to lead to completed action;
- emphasise interpersonal skills such as communication, presentation skills, stress, and time management;
- acknowledge the needs of individuals for stimulation, freedom, creativity, and fun;
- offer a variety of delivery modes; and
- be provided by people credible within the field of education, often by practitioners and consultants in partnership.

Two recommendations from this study had a direct influence on the development of the coaching model:

1. Leaders need to experience professional development in critically reflective practice, and this needs to be formalised and structured through such initiatives as professional partnerships, learning and research communities, study groups, and action learning sets.
2. Scholar-practitioners need to be made available as consultants to leaders to assist them with their professional development, to help them with problem posing, managing change, critiquing practice and political context, and to assist them with education development generally. The consultants could come from the teaching profession—the untapped source of leadership development that Wadsworth (1990) describes as a "pot of gold" in his article on the School Leaders Project.

Conversations that I had with two of the leaders who participated in the study were another major contributor to my thinking at this time. The first stated that there was nothing new in the professional development offerings and that, during his career, he had been to everything available, or at least some form of it. He also said if the development did not correspond with a "hurt" or a need being experienced by leaders, then no matter how good it looked, or was, other more pressing factors within the institution would take precedence. It seemed obvious, then, that any professional development had to focus on leaders' current leadership experience(s). The second leader had this to say: "What I would really like to do is … buddy with someone. They would spend a day or two with me, and then I would say, 'OK, warts and all, what can you see in here that I am doing wrong—tell me. What things do you like? What things am I doing that I could do better?'" I realised that this type of coaching practice was generally missing from leadership development initiatives, and that a second study was needed to pursue this line of thought. However, it also seemed to me that I needed to move this second leader's thinking away from having somebody else telling him what was wrong, to having him reflect on what might be wrong and what he might be able to do to improve the situation. This reflection and subsequent critical dialogue between the two leaders would allow him to engage more effectively in the vicarious learning he described.

The second research study

A national curriculum leadership development contract provided an opportunity to trial the use of peer-assisted learning, of the type exemplified by Barnett (1990). This time round, 44 leaders, from primary and secondary schools, were selected from their individual applications to take part. Each participant was asked to "partner" another leader during a first group session, to set goals. and to focus on their leadership role when leading learning through the curriculum and programmes. During each of four group sessions, conducted by a development team of 15 consultants and extending over an 18-month period, the partners worked together in pairs, using skills of listening, reflective questioning, and goal setting. (For a fuller description of this process, see Strachan & Robertson, 1992.) We asked the partners to think of ways of contacting each other and working together between these formal meeting times, which they did, to varying degrees. The consultants also worked with each leader in his or her school, and with the other teachers there, during these "in-between" times.

The study involved over 50 hours of face-to-face data-gathering sessions (individual and group interviews and surveys) with the 44 leaders. During the study, the leaders also completed two individual surveys designed to monitor and evaluate the issues and successes the leaders personally experienced when working in their professional partnerships. The leaders also were each sent five letters across the 18 months, reminding them of goals set from group sessions and prompting them to initiate further action and reflection with their partner.

Data from the interviews, observation, and surveys were shared with the leaders at the group sessions. This action-research process assisted with clarification and validation of emerging findings, but also intentionally influenced the continuing development process. At the end of the trial period, all data were further analysed for grounded theory development—a process described by Strauss and Corbin (1997)—to ascertain how the leaders had established and maintained successful professional partnerships throughout this time. In-depth interviews were then conducted with five volunteer participants whose coaching experiences had been relatively fulfilling, but not without issues. The aim here was to further saturate the emerging themes of data that would influence the selection and maintenance of the coaching partnerships in the third research study. This analysis took just over 60 hours.

The findings from this part of the study set the direction for the ensuing action research of the third study and firmed up the principles of the coaching model presented in this book. The findings were as follows:

1. Leaders viewed the concept of partnership coaching favourably.
2. Leaders needed improved skill development to carry out the processes effectively.
3. One year was insufficient for the coaching partnerships to develop fully.
4. Respect, honesty, and trust were important elements of a successful partnership relationship.
5. Leaders needed more in-depth outside support to assist with critical reflection on leadership practice during the coaching process.
6. Regular, sustained contact between coaching partners was necessary.
7. Leaders considered lack of time for coaching an inhibiting factor.
8. Partnerships involving leaders from institutions of similar size and type benefited problem solving.
9. Engagement in group sharing and problem posing alongside the coaching processes benefited the participants' leadership development by giving them a wider variety of perspectives and ideas.

The third research study

This third study was again qualitative, involving an action-researching community of 12 leaders and an academic researcher (myself). Over a three-year period, the leaders met regularly in their peer partnerships and as a group, and I worked with them as individuals, in their partnerships, and when they were all together as a group. The 12 leaders began by setting goals. They then used newly developed skills to observe, reflect on, and provide evaluative feedback on their own and each other's leadership practice.

A continuing influence on the development of the research and the eventual coaching model at this time was the exciting work in peer-assisted leadership development being conducted by Bruce Barnett, Ginny Lee and colleagues at the Far West Laboratory in San Francisco. Their earlier research (e.g., Barnett, 1990; Bossert, Dwyer, Rowan, & Lee, 1982; G. Lee, 1991, 1993) also had a strong influence on my developing ideas, as did Kolb's (1984) work several years previously on adult learning theory. Ginny Lee came to New Zealand and worked with the leaders in the early stages of the coaching in the third study.

By the mid-1990s, education institutions had assumed even more responsibility for their own management. My aim in this third study was to encapsulate in the coaching model a strategy of professional development that would assist educational leaders to:

- conceptualise and implement new ideas and practices;
- achieve strategic goals;
- deal effectively with current issues and problems;
- gain skills;
- develop strategies to cope with challenges; and
- receive support.

A coaching model was the obvious answer.

The research was therefore designed as a conscious effort not only to develop a theory of professional development for leaders but also, in so doing, to provide professional development that would help them understand and then change their situation at the time of the research. The underlying theoretical principle of praxis was embedded in and interwoven through my and the leaders' methods: the developing findings influenced our practice at the time of the research, and consequently how we worked with one another. The research was practical and based on the needs and concerns of the leaders involved. It was thus both a research and development model.

The study comprised 18 months of data gathering, and employed oral and written reflections, interactive interviewing, observations, and examination of records. The findings were analysed using grounded theory techniques within the methodology of action research. The processes of action research accordingly became methods for both collecting and analysing data, with both the leaders and myself jointly involved in this process as a community of researchers (after Carr & Kemmis, 1986). During the data collection and analysis, the leaders helped me explain their situation and the dilemmas and tensions they faced during coaching and in their leadership practice.

All 12 leaders testified that the coaching assisted their professional and personal development in many ways. In the words of one of them:

> This research has made me focus on my own educational leadership. It has led me through a series of processes, which have enabled me to reflect on and analyse my own actions. The research has made me take an in-depth look at my own leadership style and has given me the opportunity to observe others.

The particular ways in which these leaders believed their involvement in the research had advantaged them fell into four major categories:

1. Assisted educational leadership development.
2. Enabled critical reflection on practice.
3. Increased professional interactions.
4. Established a structure (action research) for educational review and development.

These findings are described in greater detail in Chapter 4.

Main conclusion drawn from the research

The thesis that is presented in this book thus rests on engagement with the educational leaders involved in the above and other research over the past decade as well as with many other leaders. Their collective perception is that a model of professional development involving leadership coaching, within a critical learning community, and with support and challenge from an outside facilitator, can successfully provide the essential components of professional development in which praxis and transformative practice are the desired outcomes. As an example, the leaders in the third study, when working together, created a mild disruption to their everyday practice, which led to opportunities for reflection on leadership practices. I (as a practitioner-scholar/ researcher) also assisted in this intervention process. The combination of the two—support *and* challenge—was effective in enabling critical reflection on practice and subsequent changes in practice and systems.

Are the benefits ongoing?

Research on this model of coaching has produced empirical evidence time and time again that the participants find long-term benefit from it (see, for example, T. Lee, 2002; Robertson, 2004b; Sutton, 2005; Winters, 1996). For leaders, coaching through professional partnerships is, in the short and long term:

- an effective form of professional development;
- suitable for anyone in any educational sector;
- practice based on sound research and development;
- carried out "on site" and dealing with current leadership issues and concerns;
- a chance to gain outside perspectives and feedback on practice;
- an excellent role model for leadership development in an institution;
- a way of receiving affirmation for work well done;
- an effective model for formative appraisal;
- a way of seeing how leaders' many tasks and interactions link together to form the "big picture"; and
- a framework for all other professional development activities because it is ongoing.

The research also indicates that "one-off" professional development sessions (e.g., a course or a conference) do little *by themselves* to change practice back at the workplace. Coaching provides a foundation for new growth, from ideas gained from other sources such as conferences, workshops, and seminars.

When leaders are asked directly at the end of their coaching experience if they intend to continue with their present coach or to establish a different coaching relationship in the future, they give these types of responses:

My present partnership will continue, as I believe we have both found it to our advantage. I have begun establishing another partnership with another leader in a much larger institution than mine and have found already that many issues are the same; [they] just involve differing numbers.

Yes, I will continue if my partner is willing ... I will also seek other partners for different areas of expertise.

Probably not with the same one. Personalities are very different. I hold different values.

Yes, until the end of the year [as I retire then]. Next year, if it is at all possible, I would very much like to be able to do something similar—if only in a one-way manner, perhaps with a newly appointed leader somewhere!

I hope to keep working with [partner]. My [audit] is next term, and I have invited [partner] to join me.

Yes, we will! We have not only gained professionally but also get on well together—and like the same wines!

Comments like these indicate that the practice of coaching—even the idea of multiple coaches—can be well and truly institutionalised (Fullan, 1985) as an important part of leaders' practice. If leaders do not continue with formal regular coaching once their coaching facilitator is no longer working with them, they will still have in place the skills to be more reflective about their ongoing practice. And, as a final point, if after experiencing coaching with their professional colleagues leaders generally are no longer satisfied with less in-depth relationships with other colleagues, they are more likely to try to establish professional coaching relationships with them.

SUMMARY OF MAIN POINTS

- Self-management requires new approaches to professionalism and leadership learning.
- The concept of leadership and its development is being debated internationally.
- Coaching focuses on leadership practice in context.
- Coaching is a relationship between two (or more) people committed to establishing and implementing goals and working together to achieve them.
- Coaching is most effective when coaches take a facilitative approach to learning and are open to new learning through the process.
- Coaching supports the principles of lifelong learning, capacity building, and continual improvement.
- Coaching is a dynamic process that develops uniquely to meet the changing needs of educational leaders.
- Coaching equips leaders with new professional ways of working with colleagues.
- The coaching model presented in this book is based on empirical research with leaders in many educational contexts and across many cultures and sectors. It is constantly evolving.

The concept and role
of educational leadership

CHAPTER OVERVIEW

The importance that the educational leader has in terms of the provision of effective learning opportunities is highlighted in this chapter; effective learning must be the number one focus and reason for leadership coaching. Many people think they are educational leaders but in actuality just hold a management or leadership position. This chapter endeavours to shed some light on the concept of educational leadership, and just who can exercise it. The qualities deemed important are set out and considered within the reality of a leader's work situation. The reasons why coaching is an important intervention in a leader's daily life, and how coaching can help leaders think about and respond to today's educational context are also explored.

Developing educational leadership

A transformative process

This book is not just about the process of leadership coaching but also about developing *educational leadership*—first in ourselves and then in others—through coaching leadership. Educational leadership encompasses the *informed actions that influence the continuous improvement of learning and teaching*—with an emphasis on "actions" and "learning and teaching." The primary focus is on the relationship between the two.

Caldwell (2003, p. 26) states that, "Educational leadership refers to a capacity to nurture a learning community." He goes on to say that a learning community is not necessarily a comfortable place in which to work, as there is a "hard edge to the concept" and the "stakes are high" if every student's learning needs are to be met. For Gunter (2001, p. *vii*), "Leadership is not an 'it' from which we can abstract behaviours and tasks, but is a relationship ... highly political and is a struggle within practice, theory and research. Furthermore, leadership is not located in job descriptions but in the professionality of working for teaching and learning." The word *leadership*, as used in this book, signals the energy, impetus, and collective action needed for change and improvement to occur—the word itself denotes *transformative* practice. Educational leadership is not about the position one holds, but rather the actions taken to improve opportunities for learning.

Leadership for all

All members of an education community can therefore contribute to the leadership energy needed to achieve its vision and goals. This concept of leadership, as that which can be contributed to and constructed by many "leaders" in the institution (Lambert, 1998), is synergistic, in that it is developed by those who choose to take up leadership roles. Many teachers do not view themselves as "educational leaders", even though they guide and facilitate the growth of learning for large groups of students on a daily basis. Providing effectively for learning, and the knowledge management it entails, requires educational leadership!

Caldwell (2002, p. 831) stresses that "Knowledge management involves ... developing a deep capacity ... to be at the forefront of knowledge and skill in learning and teaching and the support of learning and teaching…This is a systematic, continuous and purposeful approach that starts with knowing what people know, don't know and ought to know." Even those holding positions of responsibility do not always place sufficient emphasis on the educational leadership aspect of their role—knowing what people know, don't know, and ought to know. One of the most important roles for effective leaders, therefore, is developing leadership in others; encouraging them to take on responsibility for improving learning and achieving goals (Fullan, 2001). This is how leadership capacity is built. A "key notion in this definition of leadership is that leadership is about learning together and constructing meaning and knowledge collectively and collaboratively" (Harris & Lambert, 2003, p. 17). The effective use of coaching practices for the development of such educational leadership practice is, of course, the focus of this book. It is for leaders in education who are committed to improving pedagogy and learning. By using coaching as part of their daily practice, leaders can promote continuous leadership development and improvement of practice and, from there, effective learning in their institutions.

An underlying premise here is that education institutions that establish coaching relationships are more likely to form democratic communities of learners and therefore a special type of education culture that focuses on the continual improvement of learning. These "coaching organisations" may thus be better suited for meeting the needs of students and leaders in this knowledge age, where flexibility, innovation, and ability to adapt to change, and take on new learning are essential.

The qualities of the educational leader

Many qualities but one goal

Educational leaders are leaders who, no matter at what level in the institution, focus on improving learning opportunities as their main function, *and* work to develop their own educational leadership capacity and that of their institution. This type of leader is wanted more than ever in education today. We need leaders who can work in a complex, ever-changing educational context, who are aware of the social and political influences on their work, and who can draw on this knowledge when working with others to create necessary changes to systems and practices.

Effective educational leadership requires much more than any individual leader can attempt to do alone, and so has the potential to be greater than the sum of the individual leaders in an institution. Coaching practices drive the development of a leadership culture that produces educational leaders able to contribute collectively to the sustained and ongoing improvement of their respective institutions (Leithwood, Jantzi, & Steinback, 1999).

Educational leaders are the people in educational institutions who:

- continually search for more effective ways of facilitating learning;
- are not content with the status quo, and will act *on* as often as they act *within* the system to redesign education;
- see the importance of being transformative and innovative and encourage considered risk taking from their colleagues;
- have a strong set of values and beliefs that focuses them firmly on social justice, so facilitating their critique of policies and practices within their educational communities;
- stand out (and up) from others as people who want to make a positive difference in the lives of others, and who still believe they can;
- are enthusiastic, energetic and believe that enhancing the learning opportunities of others is central to their work and that of others;
- lead by example and model the types of practices they believe are important in the education community; and
- have developed the ability to critically reflect and to seek opportunities to develop this skill with others.

Educational leaders constantly strive for the ideal of democratic communities, where all community members assume responsibility for learning. This process is distinguished, in part, by leaders critically reflecting on the role and effect of their educational leadership, particularly in terms of building learning communities for themselves, their colleagues, students, and local business and parent communities (Apple & Beane, 1995). They value diversity yet have a sense of shared purpose. While critical reflection and thinking can be developed to some extent through the institution's learning curriculum, these practices need to be modelled in the institution's *culture*. Democracy, too, needs to be learned through the day-to-day *experiences*. As Maxine Greene (1985, p. 3) has stated:

> ... democracy is neither a possession nor a guaranteed achievement. It is forever in the making... For surely it has to do with the ways persons attend to one another, and interact with one another. It has to do with

choices and alternatives, with…the capacity to look at things as if they could be otherwise.

Coaching maximises the effect of these experiences by enhancing the learning gained from them.

Statesperson, connoisseur, and entrepreneur

Studies conducted in the late 1980s and early 1990s (see, for example, Marshall & Duignan, 1987; Robertson, 1992) grouped the qualities of educational leaders into three areas: those of the statesperson, who lobbies for the education in their institution in the wider community; those of the connoisseur, who is learned about pedagogy and committed to lifelong learning; and those of the entrepreneur, who always looks for new ways of working more effectively and innovatively so as to facilitate continual improvement of the learning experiences offered.

Leaders who are *statespeople* focus on relationships, because they know their work is with and through other people. The learning relationship is one of the most important of all relationships within an education institution, and leaders fluent in coaching practices usually have had first-hand experience of developing effective learning relationships. Teachers talk of how they approach their teaching differently after the experience of being coached. They say they hear themselves using the skills of coaching with their students to facilitate their learning processes, rather than simply teaching content and telling students what to do.

As *connoisseurs*, educational leaders focus on pedagogy—their own as a leader and that of others in the institution. Conversant with current research practices, they work to develop continual improvement in their own teaching and that of colleagues. They use evidence-based leadership (Earl & Katz, 2002; Southworth, 2002) to encourage commitment among the people they work with. They also encourage them to take ownership of issues related to improving learning opportunities within the institution.

As *entrepreneurs*, educational leaders research their own work, and that of others, and gain outside perspectives and feedback to confront their thinking. They seek out new ideas, challenges, and opportunities to improve what they do. Inventors and innovators, they like coaching because it gets them beyond the usual façade of leadership to the "nitty-gritty" of their work. They focus on problem posing as well as problem solving.

Coaching and the present-day reality of leadership

Barriers to effective leadership

As early as the mid-1980s, Apple (1986) pointed to the increasing complexity of the role of the educational leader in modern society, a situation that has intensified rather than diminished over time. The world over, reforms to educational administration and national curricula have seen educational leaders endeavouring to negotiate multiple demands on their time and cope with being pulled in many different directions. As Robertson (1995) has observed, leaders often feel they are in reactive mode, responding within a context of ambiguity, paradox, and change and to a plethora of tasks characterised by brevity, complexity, and fragmentation. Daily, they have to make choices between conflicting options raised by various issues.

According to Marshall and Duignan (1987) and Robertson (1991b), the dilemmas causing the greatest conflict for leaders are between

- the administrative and educational leadership aspects of their role;
- being accessible and being efficient; and
- decreasing authority and increasing responsibility.

Many of those in positions of leadership feel the administrative demands of their daily work limit them from exercising their leadership role within learning, and learning is what they see as their most important focus (Robertson, 1999; Wylie, 1997). Wylie (1997) identifies funding and property (building maintenance) as the two major concerns facing leaders in self-managing schools, yet the institution's educational leader should have, as their main focus, the quality of provision of learning opportunities. One leader, a newly appointed principal who participated in the research informing the development of the model, voiced his frustration in this regard: "I've really wasted a year. I've looked more at the administration side rather than at the education in the school, and I haven't pushed that side enough. That's why I am a bit nervous that I've wasted this year."

Within self-managing institutions, it would seem imperative that educational leaders are available and accessible to their communities, consulting with them over the formulation and implementation of educational goals (within nationally prescribed managerial and curricular guidelines).

However, most leaders can achieve this facet of their work only by putting in very long hours, in their own time (Robertson, 1995). Often, self-responsibility and autonomy feel a sham as they struggle to cope with an increasing raft of centrally imposed policies, innovations, and practices, a situation at seeming variance with the devolution intent of educational reforms and a product of what Codd (1990) refers to as the centrally imposed managerialist ideology on the part of government. Indeed, some educational leaders liken their role to that of a "middle manager", implementing, at the behest of others, policies for which they feel no ownership (Robertson, 1995).

This ideology also negates the intention of education policies developed to celebrate and encourage the diverse nature of the communities that schools serve. Educational leaders work with wide-ranging and ever-changing educational communities, which reflect multiple values and beliefs. Conditions in these communities' educational institutions therefore are not linear. They do not allow for clear inputs and outputs, as in, say, factories producing baked beans. Educational leaders deal constantly with the many issues, decisions, changes, and concerns that reflect the communities they serve. The implementation of a potentially transformative policy, whether nationally or locally directed, can lead to divisiveness in the community, given the multiple values and beliefs that preside there (Robertson, 1995).

The importance of critical thinking

The coaching model provides a structure whereby leaders can deal with these pressures, because it allows them to think critically and regularly about the issues as *they* experience them, and then to adapt their practice accordingly. It helps them determine if their management practice is little more than a façade, if it merely encompasses activities or ways of talking with colleagues that give the impression the institution is being well managed and is highly effective, when it may not be, as the following leader articulated:

> They were waxing loud on this—'In my institution this and in my staff... that', and 'We do this', and 'We've got that', and 'I've got this' and 'I've got that'—and I used to think, 'Holy cat fish, how will I ever become as good as they are?' And then I discovered... what I call the 'whited sepulchre syndrome'... a biblical allegory. The sepulchre is a raised tomb which you whitewash every year in memory of the death. So, on the outside, everything is beautiful, but on the inside it is all corruption.

Coaching helps leaders develop special relationships with their professional colleagues, which, as a matter of course, significantly improve professional communication within and between institutions. In the conflicts occasioned by central imposition on the one hand, and localised autonomy on the other, and by the market-driven imperatives of competition and choice, such dialogue and collaboration between leaders of different institutions can only be advantageous in terms of rebuilding collaboration and maximising the strengths of each educational institution in a community. Leaders, moreover, can become more aware of the external influences on their work and, through this understanding and the collegiality that develops, can find strategies to manage stress. They develop confidence through the coaching process, through affirmation of their work, through self-awareness and through a recognition that the role of educational leadership is complex. The support that professional colleagues offer is also vital in helping leaders to bed in the changes to practice they make as an outcome of coaching and to strive for ongoing reflection about, and improvement of, their practice.

"You tend now to really look. You really are looking for some of the things that are occurring and, when you are doing that, you are thinking to yourself all the time, 'Would I do this?'"

The need for more relevant professional development

For many leaders, attendance at their association's annual conference, the monthly meeting of the regional association or executive group, and perhaps a professional development seminar or workshop slotted in here and there when a brochure catches their attention, typifies their professional development activities (Robertson, 1991a, 1995; Stewart & Prebble, 1993; Wylie, 1994). Leaders state that they seldom, if ever, have to confront their own leadership on such occasions, and so have no impetus to change their practice when back on site. A disruption, an intervention, is often needed before change takes place. Leaders who assume the role of professional coaching partner provide this challenge for one another, as does the facilitator of the coaching process. So, too, do the members of the institution's learning community or their local network or consortium of institutions, established to support the innovation being implemented.

In similar vein, leaders rarely have opportunity to discuss educational leadership with one another or *observe* each other in practice. The term "reflective practitioner" is often more rhetoric than actuality in leaders' lives unless time is structured for the process. Coaching provides an ongoing venue wherein leaders can talk about and observe one another in action in the workplace, be it a departmental meeting, a community or business meeting, a meeting of the executive team, or time spent working on students' issues or with the board of trustees.

Over the years of my research, many people have asked what competencies, standards and/or attributes of leadership I have been intent on developing through the coaching model, and my answer has always been, "This is not a recipe approach. The model develops critically reflective leaders committed to the continual improvement of their leadership practice." The coaching model approach is the antithesis of many current leadership development trends, which Gronn (2003, p. 7) describes as the "production of leaders by design or the idea of designer-leadership." Here, sets of standards or competencies,

> *"I think you pick up a freshness, and you go back thinking, 'Oh, gee, neat, I could do something. I've seen this, or maybe I shouldn't have handled that that way.'"*

which are often culture-, context-, and gender-neutral, determine the quality or readiness of the practitioner for management positions. This preoccupation with standards and related competencies is integral to the aforementioned managerial ideology of the New Right exercised in many countries around the world, and it is at variance with an approach to leadership development researched first in Australia and then extended to New Zealand (Wildy, Louden, & Robertson, 2000) that highlights the importance of context in leadership development and practice.

I am also asked at conferences what motivated the leaders who participated in my research to take on coaching partnerships. I often answer by referring to the old adage, "You can lead a horse to water, but you can't make it drink." The answer revolves around not only how to get leaders *to* the water—which job conditions often prevent them from doing—but *how* to get them to drink once they are there. (I cover this "how to" aspect in depth in the next chapter.)

Educational leadership coaching provides an answer to these questions. Educational leaders who keep education at the centre of their work by critically reflecting on their practice are aware of the influence of managerialism on their work. They are consequently able to hold fast to their educational leadership role, and so do not become mere managers (Robertson, 1999). I believe that, without this perspective, Goodlad's words, written over 25 years ago in the USA, could become a portent for leaders in education across the world.

> We corrupted the educational process through over cultivation of the system. And now as we reflect on all this—and reflection is a luxury in which we too little indulge—we become dimly aware of something missing. That something is what motivated most of us to become teachers or educators in the first place ... to put education at the centre again, [to] want to become educational leaders again, not mere managers. (Goodlad, 1978, p. 324)

I also fear that unless this perspective comes to pervade professional development in the near future, Goodlad's words could be the lament of educational leaders 25 years hence.

> We have yielded to the pressures and temptations of becoming experts in fiscal and personnel management, public relations, collective bargaining, and the political process. Few of us are trained or experienced in any of these, even though we must take responsibility for them. What we are trained and experienced in, most of us, is education—its traditional and emerging goals, its historical roots, alternatives, curriculum, counselling, instruction. (Goodlad, 1978, p. 331)

SUMMARY OF MAIN POINTS

- Effective educational leadership can be developed through professional coaching.
- Coaching can be a reciprocal practice between peers and/or involve a learning community.
- Important qualities of an educational leader are the statespersonship of developing relations, the connoisseurship of education, and the entrepreneurship necessary to see opportunities for innovation.
- The work of an educational leader is complex and varied.
- Coaching, as professional development, acknowledges the reality of leaders' work.
- Support and challenge are essential in leaders' professional development. Coaching offers this.
- Coaching allows leaders to critically reflect on and respond to the realities of today's educational context.

Learning for leadership

CHAPTER OVERVIEW

Coaching is about seeing leadership practice as opportunities for learning. The new education context requires lifelong learning as we struggle to keep abreast of new technology, new programmes, new ideas, and new ways of working. This chapter therefore highlights the importance that lifelong learning and theories related to adult learning hold for the process of coaching. Also emphasised here are leaders' values and beliefs. These provide the "educational platform" upon which leaders base their leadership decisions. The notion that coaching helps close the gap between espoused theories of practice and leadership practice in action is also discussed here. So, too, is the idea that coaching challenges leaders to think about the theory of learning in different ways, and to recognise that, for new leadership learning to take place, leaders must cross the boundaries of their comfort zones, an experience that can be constructed through the process of coaching.

The importance of lifelong learning

Leaders who use the coaching model can develop their coaching practices in a manner that exemplifies the principles of lifelong learning. By adapting the model to their context, experience, culture, and situation leaders take responsibility for their learning and ownership of the process. Coaching is a valuable model for formative appraisal, because it focuses on improving learning experiences and opportunities over time.

Effective leadership is thus learned through experience, by those with the innate qualities that allow them to learn effectively from that experience, which is why coaching with a peer partner is crucial to ensuring *ongoing* learning of effective leadership practice. Leadership learning is then based on real experiences and actions in leaders' daily work. It is also based on reflective observation of those experiences, opportunities to question, pose and solve problems, to analyse and develop new ways of thinking and leading, and to try out new ideas. It is an essential part of the ideal of professionalism.

Uncovering the educational platform

One of the most important aspects of coaching is the coach and educational leader together clarifying the values and beliefs about education and learning on which their leadership practice and decision making rest. These values and beliefs underpin the decisions that leaders make within their institutions, and so are referred to within the context of the model as *the educational platform*.

Educational leadership requires leaders to make their values, beliefs, and interests transparent to others—to identify and articulate their educational platforms (Sergiovanni & Starratt, 2002). They need to do this for both educative and ethical reasons. The ability to draw understanding from the many actions they carry out daily depends on knowledge of these platforms, and the size of the gap between the leaders' rhetoric of espoused theories and their actual "leadership in action".

When people are asked what they would do in a certain situation, the answers they give are their espoused theories of action, which presumably govern their theories in use (Schön, 1983, 1987). However, the two do not always match, and leaders who are not aware of discrepancies or gaps between them may not see the necessity for, or be open to, new learning. Coaching helps close the gap between espoused theories and theories in action. It creates the essential conditions for "double-loop learning" to occur, which Argyris (1982, 1999) argues is essential for effective professional development. According to Agyris (1982), double-loop learning happens only when learners invite other people to observe their behaviour, so providing the catalyst that allows the learners to confront the views and values that seem to be influencing their behaviour. This is why the outside perspectives of the coaching partner are necessarily at the core of the leadership learning process.

"You are developing very independent leaders by causing them to reflect and do their own learning, and since learning is change, [to] change themselves ... I think the strength of the system is the expectation that each leader is responsible for her own development. We don't want clones."

Duignan (1989) points out that discontinuity between espoused theories and professional educative goals, principles, and values can lead to stress and tensions within daily practice. Awareness of discontinuity conversely directs attention to the possibility for positive transformation. Coaching should therefore assist leaders to understand their values and beliefs about how people learn best and what their true interests as leaders of their institutions are. It should also assist them to develop the ability to articulate their educational leadership platform in dialogue with their colleagues.

Sergiovanni and Starratt (2002, p. 71) summarise the importance of this process as "knowing *what* the platform position is, understanding the relationship between ... practices and platform elements, perceiving inconsistencies between the spoken platform and the platform in practice, [and] appreciating differences between one's own platform and that of another" (emphasis theirs). They give examples of the types of platform commonly found among educators: the basic competency platform; the democratic socialisation platform; the urban teacher platform; and the ecological platform. Most of the values and beliefs making up these platforms could belong to teachers, principals, academics, and so on, but these platforms become particularly cogent when senior leaders add in the values and beliefs they have about their role in monitoring the quality of the teaching and learning within the institution. Creating opportunities for other leaders to uncover their educational platforms is also an important role for educational leaders in positions of responsibility, and they can achieve it through collaborative "storying" during the coaching process (Sutton, 2005). Leaders therefore must be aware of the way they work daily with others, and coaching allows this. It assists them to solve the dilemmas in their leadership practice and, if necessary, change it to the advantage of those with whom they work.

Experiential learning

The exercise of educational leadership thus requires leaders to act intentionally—to strive to improve the teaching and learning experiences of those in their education communities. This desire is at the heart of praxis, which must be governed, as Duignan (1988, p. 5) reminds us, by "conscious, reflective, intentional action ... [which] is the bridge between theory and practice—between reflection, analysis and action." For leaders, opportunities to engage in this kind of action are best engendered through dialogue, observation, experimentation, and reflection on practice, in short, through experiential learning, another vital component of the coaching model.

Kolb (1984, p. 40) describes the process of experiential learning as "A four stage cycle involving four adaptive learning modes: concrete experience; reflective observation; abstract conceptualisation and active experimentation." Kolb stresses that when all four stages are given an equal weighting (see Figure 1), the outcome (desired) is effective praxis.

Experiences

Leaders' everyday work experiences, the tasks and activities they undertake, are pivotal for new learning (Kolb, 1984). Within the coaching model, professional leadership development begins when leaders make the most of an experience by carefully considering it, conducting a self-assessment, and then combining this information with feedback from the coach and others they work with to develop new principles, concepts, and theories to use on the job.

Learning out of experience not only assists with the construction of learning but also enhances intellectual independence and reinforces self-directed professional development. Self-directed learning is "a form of study in which learners have primary responsibility for planning, carrying out, and evaluating their own learning experiences ... and is the way most

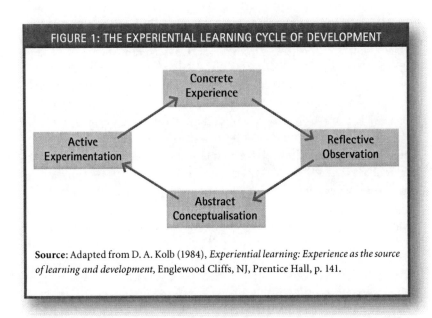

FIGURE 1: THE EXPERIENTIAL LEARNING CYCLE OF DEVELOPMENT

Concrete
Experience

Active
Experimentation

Reflective
Observation

Abstract
Conceptualisation

Source: Adapted from D. A. Kolb (1984), *Experiential learning: Experience as the source of learning and development*, Englewood Cliffs, NJ, Prentice Hall, p. 141.

adults, including professional educators, go about acquiring new ideas, skills, and attitudes" (Caffarella, 1993, p. 30).

Reflection

Reflecting on experiences and actions related to them helps leaders become more receptive to trying out new strategies and behaviours. It can also see them changing a value or a belief and, in turn, future actions. Sometimes, however, leaders do not find it easy to reflect adequately on a particular experience, and this is where coaches are so useful. Through careful questioning and prompting—direct challenge even, where warranted— they can help leaders more readily relive an experience or look at it differently (Barnett, O'Mahony, & Matthews, 2004). They can help leaders see what attitudes and values might have been making them act in a certain way at that time and to consider whether that way would be appropriate in future. "Once they [the leaders] have brought to a level of conscious awareness the strategies and values which were previously implicit, they are in a position to modify them and then to try them out again in another situation" (Candy, Harri-Augstein, & Thomas, 1985, p. 115).

Conceptualisation

Once leaders free themselves from their taken-for-granted ways of viewing the world, they can start "seriously entertaining and evaluating alternative possibilities" (Berlak & Berlak, 1987, p. 169). This process involves a type of conceptualisation wherein leaders are able to psychologically distance themselves from the issues under reflection. Working this process through with others, notably the coach, helps leaders deconstruct the dominant, prevalent discourses around these issues and the effect they are having on their role (Foucault, 1977). Leaders accordingly become aware that they are not the only ones experiencing the same difficulties and dilemmas. This gives them the confidence to find solutions to the problems rather than to expend energy blaming themselves for some perceived lack of ability.

Experimentation

Conceptualisation works best when it gives leaders the confidence to actively experiment with different concepts and ideas. Experimentation becomes the new concrete experience as the learning cycle begins again. This cycle of active experimentation is, therefore, not uninformed action but praxis: "It is this whole process of reflection-in-action which is central to the 'art' by which practitioners sometimes deal with situations of uncertainty, instability, uniqueness, and value conflicts" (Schön, 1983, p. 50). Reflection-in-action, Schön explains, "consists of on-the-spot surfacing, criticising, restructuring, and testing of intuitive understandings of experienced phenomena; often it takes the form of a reflective conversation with the situation" (1983, p. 242). If done properly, reflection-in-action becomes "knowing-in-action", because it allows people to act with confidence on the basis of informed decisions arising out of reflection on their experiences. A professional partner (coach) assists leaders to be reflective *in* action, *on* action and *for* future action, which results in a knowledge *of* practice. This process moves leadership enquiry into a new paradigm, that of leadership *as* learning.

Thinking about learning

When educational leaders become involved in systematic enquiry about their practice, whether in coaching partnerships or in professional learning communities, they gain a knowledge of practice that facilitates effective leadership. This process rests on a way of thinking about learning in order to improve leadership that is new for many educational leaders and is described by Cochran-Smith and Lytle (1999) (see Table 1). This type of thinking requires leaders to think about their work in terms of problems to be solved— to problem pose rather than just problem solve—and to be systematic about that enquiry by establishing support structures such as coaching.

Grossman, Wineberg, and Woolworth (2000) write that leaders who work together in these ways differ from other gatherings of leaders in terms of three factors important for systematic collaborative enquiry on leadership practice:

1. Commitment to colleagues' growth.
2. Recognition that participation is expected.
3. Recognition that colleagues are resources for one's own learning.

The type of thinking that supports these factors places leaders at the centre of their own learning and the responsibility for learning firmly in their

TABLE 1: NEW CONCEPTIONS OF LEARNING

New Conceptions of Learning	Differing Assumptions	Implications for Professional Development
Knowledge *for* practice	Research generates formal knowledge for use.	Dissemination of knowledge.
Knowledge *in* practice	Knowledge embedded in exemplary practice and reflection.	Focus on experience-based projects and practical knowledge.
Knowledge *of* practice	Learn by making leadership, learning, and research problematic.	Systematic and critical enquiry in communities.

Source: Adapted from descriptions given by M. Cochran-Smith & S. Lytle (1999), Relationships of knowledge and practice: Teacher learning in communities, in A. Iran-Nejad & C. D. Pearson (Eds.), *Review of research in education* (Vol. 24, pp. 251—307), Washington, DC, American Educational Research Association.

court. Leadership coaching endeavours exemplify this stance on learning responsibility.

Co-constructing knowledge

While coaching requires leaders to engage in learning partnerships with one another, the partners need not have the same values, beliefs, and ways of operating. As Elbaz-Luwisch (2001, p. 86) points out, "encounters with others who define themselves differently [allows] one … [to] participate in dialogue with many voices, a dialogue in which the self can engage in ongoing definition and redefinition." Coaching develops learning communities of leaders whose diverse perspectives on issues challenge leaders to move beyond the self to a bigger, more critical perspective on their own practice in particular and educational leadership in general (Webber & Robertson, 1998). Fullan and Stiegelbauer's (1991) belief that leaders are constrained in their learning by a ceiling effect if they keep to themselves highlights the value of dialogic encounters brought about by coaching.

"To be honest, I think I am a lot more relaxed because I know there is at least one other [person] out there who has got the same problems as me, the same hassles, the same worries, and I know that I am not unique, not the only person who has got everybody doing the wrong thing at the wrong time … some days are like that, and it's something you can ring up and laugh about."

If we believe that knowledge is constructed—as well as reconstructed—by people at both personal and group levels, a model of leadership coaching must rest on social-constructivist principles. Bell and Gilbert (1996, p. 57) support a view of learning for pre-service and in-service teacher education that takes account of how the individual contributes to the construction of socially agreed knowledge (i.e., shared knowledge developed by the group for that particular context) and of how those who have contributed to that construction then use it to reconstruct and transform the culture of the workplace and this social knowledge itself. Knowledge of empirical research and theory is important to this process. Bell and Gilbert consider that this process involves what they term "human agency"—the ability of individuals to feel that they can transform their beliefs into actions that make a difference.

Their premise is very much in line with the view of leadership learning put forward in the coaching model. Leaders experience scaffolded learning in new leadership practices in supported, authentic contexts—their own institutions. This requires a generative, constructivist approach to leadership learning, such as coaching, in which leaders focus on their own issues, as they occur, and then relate the research theory and co-constructed knowledge to their developing practice. This type of "sustained interaction produces wisdom" (Fullan, 2003b, p. 47) about leadership, about the institution and about education.

Crossing borders

Reciprocal coaching, involving shadowing (observation in the workplace) and experiences in different educational contexts, requires learners to cross over their own professionally formed "borders" and boundaries of knowledge to view how others work. Giroux (1992, p. 26) calls this crossing over "border pedagogy" and defines it as:

> ... challenging, remapping, and renegotiating those boundaries of know-ledge that claim the status of master narratives, fixed identities, and an objective representation of reality ... [and] recognizing the situated nature of knowledge ... and the shifting, multiple and often contradictory nature of identity.

Giroux argues that effective border pedagogy requires "pedagogical conditions in which students become border-crossers in order to understand otherness in its own terms" (p. 28). Leadership coaching establishes opportunities for leaders to cross borders to understand otherness, different ways of being and knowing, and how the situated nature of leadership knowledge is created. For Robertson and Webber (2000, 2002) and Webber and Robertson (1998), Giroux's notion of border pedagogy is an essential component of effective leadership-learning methodology, because it creates the conditions for "boundary-breaking leadership development" (their terminology).

Clandinin and Connelly's (1995) belief that "teachers' professional knowledge landscapes" are made up of shared stories aligns well with the concept of border crossing. Each leadership context, even within the same institution, has its own stories, its own culture of rites, artefacts, and taken-for-granted practices. It is not until leaders cross borders and share these narratives that they are challenged to critique their own leadership practices, identities, and stories. Support for this claim comes from Jasman's (2002) findings from her five research studies involving participants in a variety of border-crossing practices. Taking the border-crossing metaphor further, she identified several types of traveller: tourist, migrant, tour guide, trekker, and explorer. Each journeyed within a new knowledge territory in different ways, revealing how their amount of familiarity with and respect, trust, experience, and knowledge of the new context affected the ease with which they engaged with it and constructed new knowledge from it:

> Not only are there different borders to cross but the visa under which we travel in the other territory is an important factor in the ease of access, familiarity with, understanding of and comfort within the other territory. As with border-crossing there are rites of passage,[and] gate-keepers may subvert or ease the passage from one professional knowledge context to another. (Jasman, 2002, p. 44)

Educational institutions have many borders: between teachers and students, theory and practice, roles, departments, neighbouring institutions, institutions and communities, cultures, genders, ages, ranks, and so on. For leaders, an ability to cross these borders is extremely important, and coaching provides the means of doing this because it creates opportunities and experiences wherein leaders develop the professional skills and ways of working together that break down boundaries. In short, the skills that arise out of coaching contexts become passports for crossing borders (Jasman, 2002).

Professional development considerations

Effective coaching is based not only on theories related to adult learning but also on four elements that Fullan and Stiegelbauer (1991) have identified as important for effective professional development programmes. They are:

1. Active initiation and participation within the process.
2. Pressure and support to maintain the process long term.
3. Changing behaviour and beliefs in a manner that leads to appropriate changes to behaviour and to those changes becoming institutionalised.
4. Ownership of the change process.

Change of this kind, which leads to new learning and practices, rarely occurs by chance in an institution, and so coaching practices need to be initiated as a professional development initiative, either by one of the educational leaders or by an outside leader who has experienced coaching. When this initiation does not occur, or when it does and leaders still fail to participate, there are likely to be several reasons why.

First, people in educational institutions tend to work in relative isolation from one another (Lortie, 1975; Sergiovanni, 2001). The education profession is a lonely one when compared with the collegial interactions and culture of shared experience and observation of practice that occurs within other professions such as medicine and law. Second, leaders become so enmeshed in the "dailiness" (Griffin, 1987), routine, and habit of their everyday tasks that they rarely, if ever, have time for quality reflection (i.e., to think critically about their actions) (Barnett & O'Mahoney, 2002). Third, there is the need for others to participate in the process for critical reflection to occur (Argyris, 1982, 1999). Collegial exchange and dialogue are paramount in the adult learning process. Senge (1990, p. 59) defines dialogue as "a sharing of thoughts, feelings, and beliefs, and a suspension of commitment to a particular perspective until all available information and positions have been heard." It is this suspension of commitment that Isaacs (1999) also believes to be important to the process of dialogue. For Isaacs, effective dialogue entails four skills: listening, respecting, suspending, and voicing. Isaacs' (1999) paradigm leads to the fourth reason why critical reflection on practice is not initiated, and that is lack of skill. Many leaders do not have the interpersonal or coaching skills necessary to provide quality feedback to their peers or to reflect critically on their own practice. Educators often have not been taught how to reflect critically on their practice at any stage of their career development.

Changing leaders' habits so that they become reflective practitioners is difficult. Critical reflection cannot be achieved by reading about it. Rather, it must become a habit through use, and through reflection on that use. Critical reflection requires that the support structures, timing, and expectation of involvement commonly associated with professional development initiatives are in place first. Coaching provides this support and challenge on an ongoing basis, and offers critical reflection as one of its most important outcomes.

> *"I now question what I am doing and think, 'What would my partner think of that?'"*

- Coaching is about seeing leadership practice as opportunities for leadership learning.
- The information/knowledge-age education context requires lifelong learning.
- Articulating and understanding one's educational platform are important to leadership development.
- Espoused theories are not always leaders' theories-in-action.
- Coaching is based on maximising experiential learning.
- Coaching provides opportunities for the affirmation and validation of practice.
- A knowledge *of* practice is important for effective leadership.
- Coaching is based on a social constructivist theory of professional learning.
- Vicarious learning, through observation of others, is a very important aspect of leadership development because it breaks down barriers between and within institutions thus allowing leaders to "cross borders".
- Coaching can provide all the elements necessary for effective professional development to occur.

The value of shared learning:
Confirmation from the research

CHAPTER OVERVIEW

This chapter takes the premise that this book stands apart from many other books about coaching because its content is based on a great deal of empirical evidence gathered over 10 years of working with educational leaders in tertiary, early childhood, primary, and secondary institutions, as well as leaders in other state services and corporations. This chapter accordingly builds not only on the earlier descriptions in this book of the research that underpins the coaching model, but also on the work of other researchers and theorists, by summarising this material according to the four main ways that the model benefits leaders. It brings greater competency to leaders' educational leadership and its development. It gives leaders a greater facility to reflect critically on their practice. It increases and enhances their professional interactions, and it helps them establish the structures for action research and development. The chapter describes and discusses these advantages.

Educational leadership capability and development

Strength is gained from the *support* and affirmation that comes from working closely with a professional colleague (or colleagues) and the subsequent lessening of feelings of isolation. Support through coaching enables leaders to *focus* more directly on the *quality* of education in their institutions and on their own leadership styles and development. They become increasingly open to new ideas and *growth*, which leads to further reflection on practice and, from there, to *informed*, committed actions. In taking *ownership* for their self-development, participants gain greater intellectual independence and *agency*. They move from being reactive and isolated to being proactive and politically empowered, which gives them the confidence to improve learning opportunities in their institutions.

Support

The comment that "You are only as safe as your last board meeting" is a common statement in principals' circles. "You're damned if you do, and damned if you don't" is another familiar iteration. The precarious and dichotomous situations that many educational leaders experience in today's ever-changing educational climate often leave them feeling isolated and uncertain. The resultant loss of confidence lessens their ability to carry out their role effectively. Unless leaders experience the type of professional leadership development or support that enables them to cope effectively with change, they are likely to assume more tentative and ineffectual styles of leadership, as these comments from one leader who participated in the research attest:

> **Before coaching**: I'm always afraid, every time I stand up, just to give a few notices at meetings, or something like that. Am I going to say the right thing? Am I going to say something that someone is going to pick up on that I can't give them a good answer on?

> **After coaching**: I have gone from one extreme to the other. If I had known then what I now know, I wouldn't have let them push me about. I would have felt so empowered, supported and emancipated, that I would never have taken all that rubbish! I would have dealt with it quite differently.

Change of this sort is apparent not only in attitudes, feelings and confidence, but also in skills learned. Hargreaves and Fullan (1992, p. 7) emphasise that "Teacher development … involves more than changing teachers' behaviour. It also involves changing the person the teacher is. … Acknowledging that teacher development is also a process of personal development marks an important step forward in our improvement efforts." Coaching places leaders in a position where they no longer feel isolated. It does this by making them accessible—first to their colleagues and then to other members of the profession.

Focus

A particular benefit accruing out of the dialogue and collaboration associated with coaching is that leaders become much more willing and able to focus on their *educational leadership* role. In the absence of an approach typified by the coaching model, leaders find it much easier to focus on systems, proposal development, form filling, and finalising of budgets than on their own leadership actions. "Coaching," said one leader, "focuses us into leadership issues, and we seek evaluation. Although we may wear many hats in our institutions, we are the professional leaders [even though] sometimes … other issues can take priority."

Growth

The collaborative partnership that is implicit in coaching challenges leaders' existing thoughts and ideas in a way that heightens leaders' openness to new ways of knowing. This openness to new ideas develops over time as the trust within the coaching relationship strengthens. It is not always present in the initial stages.

The personal development that leaders experience through coaching often involves changes of approach brought about by observing alternative ways of acting. Leaders talk of new skills and ideas they pick up from visiting one another's institutions, of innovations they can immediately implement in their own institution. The new approach might be a policy or presentation for a board meeting, or involves ideas for developing a

"You need someone else to talk to—especially about specific problems. Having someone who understands these problems, can listen, can suggest ways of coping, has been a lifesaver."

strategic plan. When leaders embrace new ideas, their actions become more informed and committed. As one leader said:

> I had to think about my actions. ... [My coach's] questions, and especially her last question, "Would you do the same again?", made me think. I would handle things differently.

Informed action

An opportunity to see other leaders doing things differently, or doing things in the same manner, allows leaders to set their leadership practice in a much wider educational context. They are able to view issues and problems associated with their leadership role at both the micro level of their institution, and at the macro level of education nationally and internationally. This perspective gives them the confidence to change their previous structures and ways of working, often in a manner they may have neither expected nor envisaged. They are empowered. Their actions become more informed, more committed.

Ownership of self-development

Increased confidence and receptiveness to new ideas and growth bring with them a natural ownership of responsibility for self-development, for the necessity to effect change. Leaders consciously make changes to their leadership practice in their institutions. They recognise the importance of utilising the mentoring and instruction they gain from their coach to develop and meet their own professional goals. They draw on their coach's strengths. As areas for development are highlighted, leaders naturally seek ways to make improvements. They become more proactive within the coaching relationship, seeking out opportunities to discuss and "dissect" their practice and to engage in professional development sessions that might help them in some way. Examples from the different research studies referred to earlier in this book include:

"I now look for outside discussion with a coach. When I started, I was wary of being considered inadequate."

- attending a January course for rural school principals together;
- travelling together to a conference;

- inviting a university graduate student to facilitate dialogue between teachers in the centre; and
- initiating tertiary study groups to muse about their current research projects.

During coaching, leaders often set personal/professional goals and ask their coach and others for evaluative feedback on these areas of focus. Some coaching partners choose to have their coach observe them taking meetings, or to watch as they conduct appraisal interviews with their staff. Others may ask their coach to observe them during strategic planning sessions, or at meetings of the board. Education consultants and facilitators who are coaches, but also have coaching partners, sometimes conduct consultancy projects together with their coach, setting goals for improvement of consultancy and giving specific feedback on resultant consultancy practice.

"I needed some honest feedback. I didn't feel the least bit threatened.
I asked his opinion of how I gained co-operation from the staff and how he felt relationships were."

Agency

When leaders realise that they do not have to continue practising as they have previously, they experience agency; they feel sufficiently freed and empowered to take alternative actions. Agency was seen when one of the leaders (newly appointed to his position) benefited from the previously learned experiences of another more experienced leader:

> I was new and ... fairly gullible. I would have taken it all on, but when I heard [partner] say that, I thought, "Cripes I don't have to do that!" ... I list things more now ... that they have to do.

Agency also helps leaders present a united front on issues. A senior leader in one of the research studies saw this as a particular benefit of developing a professional partnership with a colleague. His presence at one of her senior staff meetings lent valuable support as she discussed with staff the issue of implementing mandated policy relating to senior staff performance agreements.

> I could see that such a situation could be useful for a leader wanting to gain support for unpalatable policies if the leaders prepared themselves beforehand.

Critical reflection on practice

Coaching builds capable leaders by enabling them to bring critical reflection to their leadership practice. Through involvement in coaching, leaders gain practical experience of and skills in utilising reflection in, on, and for practice. They come to recognise that reflection is a powerful tool for enhancing the quality of leadership actions in their work.

Reflection

The importance of reflection on practice, and ensuring that it occurs, has been well noted in this book. Being reflective is an essential quality of good leadership, and is one that needs to become embedded in the culture of the institution. One leader commented that reflection arising out of her ongoing commitment to collegial coaching had become a "fully accepted ... part of this institution." She now included the coach and partner institution in activities and decisions made, and in the consultation process for future planning.

Structure

Reflection that leads to agency rarely occurs naturally in leaders' practice. While leaders may recognise that reflection is important, they find it difficult to put aside time within the day for critical reflection. Reflection time therefore needs to be structured, so that it is formalised into the busyness of leaders' days. The coaching model teaches leaders how to take the time to reflect on their leadership performance and their proposed actions. Structured time enables leaders to become increasingly reflective about what they are doing or are planning to do.

Vicarious learning

Because the coaching model involves reciprocal processes, leaders gain benefit from reflecting not only on their own practice but also on their coach's leadership actions within their practice. The time that the model makes available for the coaching partners to observe each other's actions becomes enforced time for reflection on practice. Leaders are able to stand back from the demands of the day and think about their own practice as they observe their coach in action. Here, they are learning about leadership vicariously.

The leaders who participated in the research valued this aspect of coaching, with most saying they had seldom, if ever, watched a leader, in a similar position to their own, carry out their work. They spoke of "freshness", of "taking away ideas", each time they worked with their coaches in this way.

Challenge

When leaders are given opportunities to observe the leadership practice of others, they are challenged by what they see. They develop doubts and questions about their own work. They begin to problem pose about it, and in so doing develop new ways of "knowing" and of "being". Reflecting through coaching does not always lead leaders to change their own practice, though. Often, consideration of another leader's practice affirms them in the way they are operating. Leaders' styles are different in different contexts, and coaching is effective here because it is not about one leader telling another leader how they should lead, but about one leader assisting another leader to think critically about their practice.

> *"Shadowing my coach makes me think about what I am doing, ways I could do things differently. It is just so neat for me to have the chance to watch you and to think how would I act or what would I have done ... I learn so much."*

Perspectives

The reason why leaders are challenged by their observations of the practice of others is that it gives them different perspectives on how leadership actions are, and might be, done. One leader described the value of different perspectives as "a pair of eyes coming in from out." He felt that the fresh perspectives that his coaching partner had brought to him would help shorten the time he had originally set to achieve certain goals. Different perspectives not only help leaders become more critical of their own leadership practice but also more knowledgeable about the values and philosophies that underpin their practice. They are also essential for double-loop learning, where reflection and feedback on previous actions inform and perhaps change future practice, thereby creating knowledge for action (Argyris, 1999).

Praxis

Many times in the coaching process, leaders become aware that their espoused theories are not the same as their theories-in-action. It is when they become more critically aware and informed of their actions, through the receiving of feedback from their coaching partner and others, that they think more carefully about the effects their actions are having on the quality of learning in their institution. They ask, states Smyth (1991, p. *xviii*), these questions: "What am I doing? What are my reasons? What are the effects of my actions on my students?" It is at this point that their practice moves to praxis, with their leadership, of itself, providing opportunities for learning and, in turn, enhanced professionalism.

Increased professional interactions

The many ways in which professional interactions can be enhanced through coaching depend on how the practice of coaching is established in an institution or between groups of leaders. These interactions can be between peers; between institutions and other members of staff in the institutions; between the members of a group, network, or community of leaders; and between an outside facilitator, researcher, adviser, or consultant, and the leaders themselves.

"We are terribly critical people. When anyone says anything [wrong or untoward], we don't overtly do anything, but we think a lot ... we are all very critical of each other and jealous of our own patch and our own domain."

Between partners

As leaders become increasingly conversant with coaching, they begin to reflect on the differences between their interactions within their coaching partnership and/or their coaching group, and their usual interactions with colleagues at other times. These "other times", they say, are characterised by talk that is more social than professional, or by discussions that focus more on systems and organisation-based features of their institutions than on resolving specific leadership dilemmas that arise within them. They speak of an unspoken rule, that of not revealing personal concerns or feelings of inadequacy—of upholding the belief that they are managing well.

Goffman (1959) has described this stance as *impression management.* We might describe it as the professional façade that leaders employ, both with their colleagues and with the outside world. (The leaders in the research studies observed that colleagues rarely revealed anything of depth when they talked together in their usual social and professional situations.) Groups of like-minded people, such as educational leaders, maintain the façade whenever they get together through rules and rituals they have established for "usual" behaviour. Should someone break these traditions, it is explained away as a *faux pas,* a communication breakdown, or similar. The members of the group support and portray a view of themselves that they know others will find, at least temporarily, acceptable. Their message is: "We are all finding the job easy. Our institutions are running well. We are keeping up with everything." This "bluff exterior" or "veneer of consensus" is, according to Goffman (1959, p. 21), the means by which they conceal their own needs.

The coaching model research shows that, with the right opportunities, leaders can get beyond the veneer of consensus to reveal their own professional needs, gain a deeper understanding of themselves and one another, and from there work towards the development of quality leadership development. Coaching gives a "pause for thought"; it interrupts accepted ways of interacting with colleagues and frees the participants to engage in new and more fruitful interactions. This freedom gives leaders the confidence to share things with their coaches that they had thought they would never share with other colleagues, although sometimes the degree to which they lay themselves open to their partner's critique concerns them. For example, when one leader invited his coach to observe his visit with an audit team, he was as concerned about seeming inadequate in front of his professional colleague as he was about appearing inadequate in front of the team:

> *"It is easy to see these things in other people. It would be interesting to know what my coach thinks of the way in which I attempt to manage ... I suppose I am just a different sort of person."*

> [My coach] said he was impressed with the fact that I clearly knew [his institution], knew the staff and knew the programmes that were going on within it. So that was good, because, between ourselves, that was the thing that worried me. I didn't want to look silly—not only in front of them but in front of a colleague.

Feeling secure enough to display vulnerability and a lack of surety with colleagues takes time, but once that point is reached, many advantages follow. Receptiveness to constructive feedback, to considering and accepting the need for change, is an obvious one. But there is also the support that comes from sharing problems and concerns—of not feeling alone, of knowing that others feel the same way. With time, collegial partners also give more of themselves, in terms of wanting to help their partner. They share ideas, exchange new resources, note down ideas, become more enthused about what they do. Their meetings and observation visits are punctuated with such questions as: Have you seen this? Have you done that? What have you done about this? What do you think of this? Would this work?

Between institutions and within institutions

When coaching relationships are established between two leaders from different institutions, there is often a flow-on effect to the other professional relationships within the institution and between the institutions. As leaders become more familiar with one another's institutions and contexts, they begin to identify the strengths in each other's practice and to look for ways in which they can share this valuable resource.

The philosophy of collegiality that two principals in one research study fostered through working closely was pervasive throughout the culture of their schools. The role models they were portraying to their staff, and their belief in the value that openness to professional development and lifelong learning would have for improving education in their schools, paved the way for increased collegial and collaborative interactions between individual members of their staff. One principal identified the importance of the role model he was setting very early on in one research study:

> I think it is important that the staff see that the principal is also committed to the concept of professional development and that the principal doesn't think, 'Well, I'm at the top—now you others catch up!'

For this principal, being the principal learner in his education community was the most important facet of his educational leadership role. Coaching helps leaders establish this type of role model.

Within a learning community

Developing relationships with other leaders who are involved in professional coaching builds learning communities. This is especially so when the regularity and quality of professional interactions between individual sets of coaching partners are such that a climate of trust and professionalism is engendered. The development of an ethos of trust in the group is one of the outcomes of coaching, and for the following leader was evident in a lack of hierarchy:

> There are the ones starting off, the others retiring. There is a good atmosphere of sharing, and it certainly never comes to me at any time that the experienced ones have the answers. If anything, it is some of the young ones in the less experienced positions who tend to feel they have the answers and are certainly innovative in the way they attack problems … For me, there are two distinct groups involved, and neither feels dominated by the other, and each is prepared to learn from the other.

Because trust takes time to develop, it cannot be assumed, and may require careful facilitation by the members of the learning community or by someone selected to provide a facilitative role. Nonetheless, comments like that made by the leader immediately above confirm the reciprocity that arises from a spirit of trust. A recognition that colleagues act as a learning resource and a receptiveness to new learning are important principles of the coaching model. A group diverse in terms of gender, ethnicity, experience, and type of institution provides the many different perspectives needed to challenge thinking about leadership issues within individual coaching partnerships.

"It will be necessary to set up some system [of] confidentiality when we talk in the larger group. I don't think there's any problem between coaching partners … but I don't know the other participants, and I'm sure that we all need to feel secure in what we have to say."

Between coaching partners and outside facilitators

The research on coaching partnerships over the years demonstrates that the presence of facilitators operating as scholar-practitioners and/or researchers in the coaching process is not only welcomed by participants but also strengthens the reflexive nature of the model. Both participant and facilitator experience an increase in useful interactions between their respective communities, something they rarely expect. Both gain from the perspective of the other and draw together in a way that sees each person contributing to and benefiting from the research process. In short, they move towards becoming a community of researchers (Carr & Kemmis, 1986). However, as various studies have shown time and again, the two parties to what is essentially an action research process (i.e., cycles of related actions based on reflection, evaluation, and evidence) retain as their primary focus their own sphere of interest. As Somekh (1994) has put it, such collaborators generally simply inhabit each other's castles, with the educational leaders always more interested in how they can use the outcomes of the research to improve their practice and their institution, and the scholar-practitioners/researchers more interested in how practice confirms and informs theory and is driven by it.

> *"We need you here though—to keep us focused on leadership, as that is ... the hardest thing to do; systems and management are the easiest things to focus on."*

Leaders often act differently in their coaching partnerships in the presence of an outsider, but this effect can be used to change practice. One leader thought third-party feedback should be built into the coaching model on a permanent basis:

> I have begun to wonder about the value of groups of three, since skill in causing another to reflect needs careful honing and should be the highlight. A third person could give feedback on the interview.

This example also points to how the practitioners themselves help develop the theory behind the professional coaching model. The model as originally conceived saw the leaders becoming autonomous through coaching. However, it became increasingly apparent that an outside facilitator could bring to the reflection aspect of the model the added dimension of research theory and other relevant matters, such as the political context within which education operates. This contribution made for a very valuable modification to the model.

The coaching model is, therefore, enhanced by the input of a facilitator, by somebody who can challenge, give feedback on the developing processes, and keep working to extend the skills of critical reflection. The facilitator can thus improve the quality of the professional coaching relationship. He or she can also keep the practitioner "on track". Often, leaders neglect critical reflection because of the demands of the management issues they face daily. The facilitator can challenge them in a way that returns them to their educational leadership role. An outside facilitator is often the person best suited to bring about the type of critique that leads to the professional transformation that Dempster (2001) calls for.

A framework for research and development

Coaching establishes a framework for the development of collaborative action research processes that lead to personal, professional, and institutional transformation. The depth of these transformations was one of the leadership developments most evident in the data gathered in the research studies. The ongoing relationship with a colleague that coaching provides helps leaders formalise a process to achieve their goals. This is because the colleague-as-coach keeps leaders' firmly focused on their leadership actions and encourages them to monitor how these influences progress towards their goals. This type of focus, it seems, is the one most likely to produce consistent, reliable change. Exactly how the action research nature of the coaching module works in this regard is the subject of the next chapter.

> ### SUMMARY OF MAIN POINTS
>
> - Coaching leads to enhanced critical reflection on practice.
> - Coaching emphasises the educational leadership role.
> - Increased professional interactions are an important outcome of coaching relationships.
> - As a result of collaborative engagement with others through coaching, leaders focus on how their learning informs their educational practice, and the impact this has on improvement and innovation in their institutions.
> - Coaching establishes processes and practices for action research and education development, which helps bed in long-term positive change.

Action research
and coaching

CHAPTER OVERVIEW

When leaders set long-term goals and begin to work surely and consistently towards those goals by monitoring progress, reflecting on and evaluating actions, and developing new plans of action in the light of that reconnaissance, they have moved into cycles of action research. This chapter outlines how action research is closely aligned to the process of coaching. It begins with a brief definition of action research. This is followed by a look at the theoretical construction, principles, and methodology of action research. The way in which action research operates within the framework of the model of leadership coaching is then outlined. The chapter ends with a case study of how two principals aligned action research and coaching to achieve a shared vision for their schools.

Action research defined

Action research is a process involving cycles of action, which are based on reflection, feedback, evidence, and evaluation of previous actions and the current situation. Data are gathered, and these inform future decisions and actions. This type of research is favoured by people who want their research findings to have an impact on the situation or context as the intervention takes place, and it sees the practitioner as researcher. The process of research and action thus results in people using the "findings" of the action research— the theory—at the time of the research. "Action learning" is closely aligned to, and indeed is part of, action research. However, with action research (or "theory of practice"), close links are made between theory and practice, and the findings are often shared in a written form.

Theoretical constructs

Action research can be traced back to the sociological work of Kurt Lewin (1948). Lewin believed that it was not only important but ethical that emancipation and change were the direct and immediate outcomes of research processes. He observed that although people are often very clear about the "what" outcome they hope to achieve when conducting research or development projects, they tend not to be so clear about *how* to reach that point. The action research process is extremely powerful in allowing them to do this.

The process begins, according to Lewin (1948), with the researcher setting down a "general idea" of what he or she wants to achieve, for example, "Develop a learning community" or "Develop a conductive education philosophy". The next step involves gathering information about the present situation, which allows the researcher to formulate "an 'overall plan' of how to reach the objective, and [to make] a decision in regard to the first step of action" (Lewin, 1948, p. 205). This stage is followed by a series of phases, each involving "circles" of action, evaluation, reflection, fact finding, modifying the original plan and planning the next action. Lewin likens the process to a spiral staircase, where the steps ultimately lead to the achievement of the desired outcome.

Lewin's (1948) description of action research has particular resonance with the coaching processes used to facilitate effective leadership. As Oja and Smulyan (1989, p. 9) state, action research provides educationists with opportunities "to gain knowledge and skill in research methods and applications and to become more aware of options and possibilities for change [and to] become more critical and reflective about their own practice." Many other theorists and researchers propound action research as a powerful means of building learning communities and influencing practice (see, for example, Cardno, 2003; Fullan & Stiegelbauer, 1991; Kemmis & McTaggart, 1988). One of the major benefits of action research is that the practitioners not only pose the research questions but search for and try out their own answers to those questions. Because the research is practitioner driven, it promotes the development of professionals and the body of knowledge on which they base their actions. In today's rapidly changing educational climate, it is important that leaders study their own practice and construct the new knowledge needed to answer their current questions and solve their own problems.

Guiding principles

The guiding principles of action research appear over and over in the literature. These principles posit action research as an intervention, as self-evaluative and collaborative, as site based and concerns based, as transformative, and as agentic (i.e., acting with agency). Another principle is that action research provides a link between theory and practice.

Intervention

Like action research, coaching is an intervention because it requires people to stop and look critically at the reality of their worlds. For Cohen and Manion (1980, p. 174), the benefits of action research come from "a close examination of the effects of ... intervention", of reflecting on the information "thrown up" by the intervention, and then determining how understandings elicited from that reflection can be used to advantage personal and professional development and practice. They go on to say that action research as intervention involves several key components:

> [It is] ... *situational* ... concerned with identifying a problem in a specific context and attempting to solve it in that context; it is usually ... *collaborative*—teams of researchers and practitioners work together on a

project; it is *participatory*—team members themselves take part directly or indirectly in implementing the research; and it is *self-evaluative*—modifications are continuously evaluated within the on-going situation, the ultimate objective being to improve practice in some way or other. (emphasis original)

There is some dissension in the literature as to whether the intervention aspect of the action research process should focus on an issue, problem or assessment of current practice (see, for example, Alcorn, 1986; Kemmis, 1985) or on a desired goal (see, for example, Lewin, 1948). As Winter (1989, p. 13), asks, "Do you start by implementing a change? Or do you start by analysing current practice in order to formulate a desirable change?" He answers these questions with another: "Does it matter which comes first?" My research has demonstrated that when educational leaders undertake action research as part of the coaching process, they generally start with the vision they wish to achieve for the development of their institution.

Self-evaluation and collaboration

The practitioner-as-researcher aspect of action research is deemed an intrinsic *part* of the "general ideal of professionalism" (Winter, 1989, p. 4) for educational leaders, rather than as an addition to it. There is an assumption here that, in their research role, leaders become "capable of determining their own performance on the basis of self-reflection" (Elliott, 1991, p. 27). They also contribute to the development of a critical learning community when they come together to explore their new learning and understandings and to share their experiences (Robertson, 2000). "The possibilities for critical self-reflection and critical collaboration should not be bypassed ... if those involved truly wish to initiate change and sustain improvement" (Cardno, 2003, p. 25).

Site based and concerns based

Action research is site based because it is carried out where the leader is actually working rather than on an island of professional development some place removed. It is concerns based because it focuses on the issues and difficulties that arise in everyday practice.

Transformative and agentic

Action research is a particularly powerful tool for professional and institutional development because it leads people to a point where their actions are informed by new understandings (transformation) and a desire to improve the conditions in which they are working or living (agency). They come to see that they can act otherwise, and they have a heightened sense of self-efficacy. Action research fulfils Fullan's (1993) call for educationists not only to base their practice on a strong value system but also to be change agents within their institutions. This is how, he says, they become transformative rather than reproductive agents of existing social patterns.

Carr and Kemmis (1986), in focusing on the emancipatory power of action, take a similar stance. They stress the need to "develop a systematic understanding of the conditions which shape, limit and determine action so that these constraints can be taken into account" (p. 152).

The words of these researchers have particular implications for educational leaders who undertake action research. For them, such research must involve critiquing the societal and political contexts in which their leadership is being carried out. The research must allow them to view matters from a variety of perspectives—to have "the capacity to look at things as if they could be otherwise" (Greene, 1985, p. 3). In this regard, leaders engaged in action research to effect change in their institutions need to seek out diverse opinion so that not only are the most dissonant voices *heard* but the responses are actively *sought* (Fullan, 2001).

Link between theory and practice

The coaching model outlined in this book is based on the precept of theory informing practice and practice informing theory. This link between theory and practice is important for the development of an education theory that "fits" the complex, constantly evolving context in which educational leaders work. It also aligns well with the development process in action research, which endeavours to lessen the gap between espoused theories and theories-in-action—to "transform...the situation from what is, to something...better" (Schön, 1983, p. 147). This consideration does not imply a rejection of all *a priori* theory, but an understanding that theory and practice must be linked for "both the advancement of science and for the improvement of human welfare" (Whyte, 1991, p. 8).

There is some disagreement as to whether action research as described thus far constitutes real action research. According to Stenhouse (1975), research can only be called research if its findings are made public. Ebbutt (1985, p. 157) concurs, stating that "if action research is to be considered legitimately as research, then participants in it must be prepared to produce written reports of their activities." Kemmis and McTaggart (1988) take a contrary view. They argue that because action research assists participants to improve what they do, there is no need for them to write up and disseminate their work: "… action research provides a way of working which links theory and practice into the one whole: ideas-in-action" (p. 6). Oliver (1980) also sits on this side of the debate, claiming that the purpose of action research is "to promote a continuing process of professional development" (p. 395). Robertson (2000) holds more the middle ground, demonstrating in her research that there can be action research for theory and action research for action.

Another facet of the theory versus practice debate is whether practitioners can develop theory. The answer to this rests on the belief in the credibility and importance of the professional knowledge—the theory—that practitioners create through their practice (Argyris, 1982, 1999; Schön, 1983; Sergiovanni, 1991). It is this type of professional theory and knowledge—or, more particularly, co-constructed knowledge developed through critical reflection on practice and related information—that is essential in a rapidly changing leadership context. Coaching validates practitioner theory development.

Action research in action

Within the framework of leadership coaching, action research involves several steps. These are identification of a need or vision and the related goal setting, gathering data, developing an initial action plan, implementing action, reconnaissance on that action, modification of the action plan, and then further agreed action. The last step provides the beginning step for a new cycle of research, and the process continues in this cyclical way until the leader achieves the desired outcome. The role that the coach (as critical friend) plays in this process is detailed on the following pages.

The cycle is presented in diagrammatic form in Figure 2. The representation draws on the conception of action research that developed out of the research studies. It also is premised on the action research processes described originally by Lewin (1948), particularly the notion that although practitioner-researchers start with a perceived outcome, how they will get there cannot necessarily be pre-identified. Within the coaching framework, it is the reconnaissance after each action that helps leaders decide what step(s) to take next.

a) Needs identification and goal setting

This step begins with leaders identifying a need or vision arising out of their practice and then articulating that need or vision in terms of a goal they wish to achieve. The goal should be stated as a succinct statement that provides direction for the action research. When setting research goals, educational leaders need sufficient time to think about and define exactly what it is they want to achieve with their coach. Here are some examples of goals that leaders have set:

"At the end of this session I find myself thinking about the next step, the goals I want to achieve..."

- To lead the staff positively through the upcoming review.
- To standardise assessment throughout the institution.
- To develop a five-year education plan.
- To establish resource-based learning across all rooms.
- To develop the institution's profile so that there is ownership by faculty, council, and senior management.
- To lead my staff into the area of data gathering in a non-threatening way.
- To set a better system of appraisal in place.

b) The initial plan

Setting a goal is one thing. Reaching it is another. The initial plan allows leaders to bridge the gap by setting out the means and methods whereby they will carry out their actions. The plan usually includes gathering data to gain a better understanding of any issues relating to the achievement of goals or to help point out future directions for action. Here are some examples of first steps leaders might take:

- Coaching partner will first observe me take a staff meeting and then assist me in getting all staff on board.
- Look at areas such as organisation of time (class, staff, administration, secretarial, cleaning, environment).

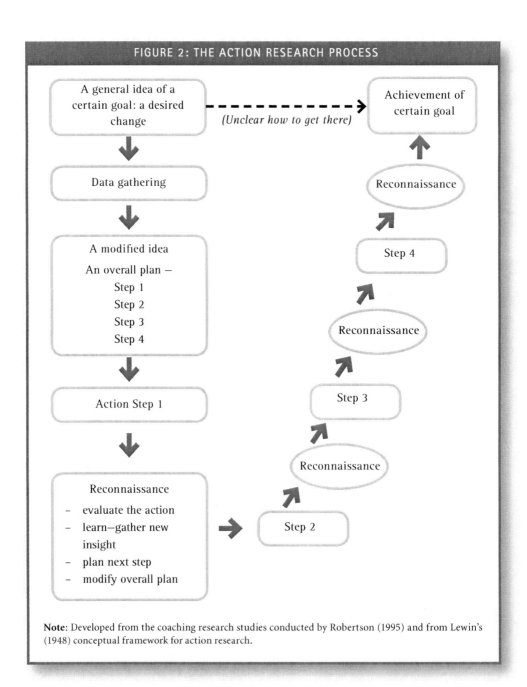

FIGURE 2: THE ACTION RESEARCH PROCESS

A general idea of a certain goal: a desired change

(Unclear how to get there)

Achievement of certain goal

Data gathering

A modified idea
An overall plan –
Step 1
Step 2
Step 3
Step 4

Action Step 1

Reconnaissance
- evaluate the action
- learn–gather new insight
- plan next step
- modify overall plan

Step 2

Reconnaissance

Step 3

Reconnaissance

Step 4

Reconnaissance

Note: Developed from the coaching research studies conducted by Robertson (1995) and from Lewin's (1948) conceptual framework for action research.

- Interview each staff member separately to get agreement on performance agreement contracts.
- Hold one-day workshop for deans to develop initial ideas for profile document.
- Month 1: Set up meeting. Involve board and community members.

c) First action and reconnaissance

Leaders then carry out the first action of their plan. (In the coaching situation, this may occur with or without the observation and feedback of the coach.) They then reflect on the outcomes of the action and decide what direction(s) to take from there (reconnaissance). Those directions may require modification of the ensuing steps in the initial plan.

d) Second and subsequent actions

Leaders now move on to their second action and period of reconnaissance and plan modification. They continue this process until they arrive at, or near, the desired outcome.

Coaching action research

The collaborative nature of coaching is a key feature in leading leaders into action-research processes. Coaches, as critical friends, help to keep their partners focused and moving systematically ahead to achieve their goals. Leaders can all too easily get sidetracked by the minutiae of their everyday work, which limits their ability to assess progress towards goals.

Coaching reminds leaders to monitor their action plans and related time frames. Coaches also keep their partners firmly focused on the bigger picture of education and leadership, rather than on the management tasks that make up much of their day.

The leaders involved in the research studies were quite specific about how their respective coaches could assist them with feedback. Examples include the following:

- Monitor introductory process and see if goals are clear.
- Evaluate the degree of change.
- Assist with evaluation through reflective interviews with staff.
- Observe an executive team meeting.

One leader said the best way her coach could assist her was to act as her conscience. The goal she had set herself was a personal one: "To see something through to the end."

AN ACTION RESEARCH CASE STUDY:
Coaching towards a shared vision

The following case study describes the collaborative, consistent approach that two principals took to achieve the same outcomes for their individual schools. They regarded their coaching partnership as equal give and take at all times and felt that they both benefited from the processes of collaborative action research. These two principals continued their coaching relationship over a four-year period. The case study has been adapted and abridged for this publication so that only Mary's story is told. For the full version, see Robertson (1995).

Year 1
The developing partnership

Mary was moving into her first year of principalship when she saw advertised a one-year programme offering the support and development of school leaders. She applied and was selected. At the first session, the 42 leaders present were paired with another leader in the group as their "partner and coach" for the professional development during the year. (Leaders were given as much personal choice of partner as was possible within the constraints of pairing up a large group.) Mary had not met her partner, Laura, before this meeting, and she later said of it: "Very surface level sharing took place. Very safe territory—factual sharing of information only."

Over the next three months, Mary commented on the process of developing a professional, working relationship with her partner: "Slowly and unobtrusively, a partnership and trust is developing." As the trust developed, so did the desire to work together on professional issues such as the appraisal of themselves and their staff. As the two principals began to recognise the value of sharing ideas and issues with a professional colleague, the sharing became more productive.

The beginnings of action research

Mary began to reflect about her school. "I began spending time at the course thinking: 'Is our school effective? How do we know this? How can we show this?'" She developed a general idea of a goal that she wanted to achieve. "I wanted a shared vision for the school; to develop an education plan owned by the staff, children and community." At this stage she was not clear as to the specific steps she would take to achieve this.

YEAR 2
Data gathering

Mary began gathering data relevant to her area of interest. She spent time looking at other schools' long-term plans and discussing her developing ideas with Laura. She reread previous course notes on development plans and talked informally with staff and her board of trustees. Mary had four excellent staff members, but sometimes felt that they were all working in different directions. If they could all work together towards a common goal and vision, she felt the whole school would then be so much greater than the sum of its five individual parts. Mary located an article on shared vision and total quality management principles that echoed her sentiments and gave her ideas.

Refining the goal

Mary refined her original series of questions to these questions: "What type of children should leave Cloverleaf [pseudonym] School? What knowledge, skills, attitudes, ideas, values, should they have? Are we all working to the same end?"

Establishing the overall plan

Mary's next step was to develop a one-year plan of action towards her goal of developing a shared vision for the school. Her plan identified curriculum areas to focus on as a school, as well as other aspects affecting the school. The plan included professional development, staff meetings and community surveys. The first action Mary put down on her plan was to hold a full staff meeting.

Action

During the staff meeting, discussion centred on methods of monitoring assessment in the school. Questions like "What are we doing? How do we know our children are being successful?" were beginning to be asked.

Reconnaissance (evaluating the action)

In evaluating the outcomes of her first action—the staff meeting—Mary quickly realised none of the teachers had the whole picture of a child's progress at and through Cloverleaf School. Each was focusing on his or her one small part in the process and had no particular conception of the desired outcome of the entire process. This lack of clarity meant that the school was not accountable for the children's learning.

New insights

From her reflections, Mary decided with the teachers that they all needed to become far more aware of what was happening in each other's rooms as well as the beliefs and philosophies that each of them held. She talked to each teacher separately and tried to understand more fully herself what was happening in each classroom. Mary talked to Laura about whether she felt her teachers were also working in relative isolation. As her coach, Laura was a constant source of outside perspectives and support, and she acted as a facilitator of the review and development process throughout this time.

Mary and Laura continued to practise the skills of observation of leadership actions, giving feedback, and conducting reflective interviews. They also spent one week of their May holiday break together and attended the rural school principals' conference. Mary found herself still reviewing previous notes on school vision and school achievement, and discussing these ideas with Laura and other colleagues.

Modification of the initial plan

Mary then decided that the next step should be to allocate one entire day to the professional development of teachers. She modified her original plan to include this day of consultation and sharing.

Action

For the teacher-only development day, Mary set up an individual folder for each staff member. The material in it outlined and summarised the main points she had taken on each of the principals' courses she had attended and provided ideas for developments in the school. She invited the mathematics advisers and an academic researcher to spend different parts of the day with the staff and to provide outside perspectives on their discussions. The staff shared with one another their own assessment and evaluation systems for the different curriculum areas. Mary introduced the idea of a portfolio for each child that could follow the child through each of their years at the school and that highlighted their development in each curriculum area. Much debate and discussion on the issues followed.

Reconnaissance

This development day led Mary into another period of reconnaissance and refinement of the overall goal. She decided that the key question arising out of the development day should set the wording of it: "What do we want children leaving Cloverleaf School to have achieved?" She then decided to gather more data, and to this end asked each staff member to answer the question in relation to each of the curriculum areas. Mary typed up their responses and then talked to Laura and other principals and the school advisers to get ideas about what was happening in the development of curriculum objectives in other schools.

Action

Mary took the collated results of the questionnaire along to the next staff meeting, and these were discussed with considerable interest. "Discussions were held on some items identified, some we wanted removed, some we hadn't thought about and had overlooked." One of the key questions that arose at this meeting started the next phase of reconnaissance: "What do parents want for their children? Are our goals and perceptions the same?"

Reconnaissance

During this period of reconnaissance, Mary spent time talking with Laura about future actions and past actions. The two women then approached another school leader in the coaching group for advice and assistance. He invited them to visit his school to view the way evaluations were conducted and recorded in the junior school. Mary began to reflect that the one-year plan she had initially set down would not be long enough to achieve the objective she desired. Her original idea of a five-year plan would be much more realistic. She again modified her plan, deciding as her next action step to send the same questionnaire, with supporting explanations, home to the parents to gauge their views.

Input from observing researcher

It was at this point that the researcher observing Mary and Laura's coaching partnership stepped in. The researcher considered that although action research was occurring, very little in the way of action plans was actually being written down. She initiated a discussion with the two women about the action research processes taking place. Both were very interested to see how the theory of the process and principles of action research matched what they were currently doing, as they had not realised that they were "action researchers". Mary then wrote down the next six months' actions and put an asterisk besides the items where she felt her coach could best assist by shadowing (observing) her and giving her evaluative feedback. "I wanted my partner's help to achieve my goals by keeping me on track, checking dates [were] being met, watching a staff meeting to see if I'm selling the overall idea to the staff, that they have ownership too, [and] observ[ing] board of trustees' reaction to the ideas at a meeting."

Further modification

Mary and Laura then worked together to collate the community survey returns and typed a summary to present to the staff at the next meeting. Once again, as a result of evaluating previous actions, learning new insights and planning future actions, along with discussions with her coach and the researcher, Mary modified her original plan.

POSTSCRIPT

The coaching went on for another year, during which Mary continued to develop, in accordance with her five-year plan, her vision of two and a half years previously. Throughout the third year, Mary and Laura's professional coaching partnership helped them support each other in their personal, professional, and school development processes, and allowed them to gain sound skills to assist each other to reflect upon their leadership practice in their schools.

During their time together, the two leaders were able to "cross-credit" their learning of the skills of coaching and the skills of action research. For example, in learning how to conduct reflective interviews, they learned to ask in-depth questions of each other, enabling them to reflect on what they were doing, why they were doing it and what effect their actions had on learning. Mary and Laura were also able to refine their ability to observe leadership behaviours and describe and evaluate these as a valuable basis for reflection. Perhaps, most importantly, they learned to act in the capacity of an outside facilitator, nudging each other along, challenging each other, affirming and supporting each other and, above all, helping each other to redefine goals, develop steps in the action research process, and reflect upon the outcomes.

While working with Laura, Mary kept notes of the process her school was working through to achieve the desired outcome, and its progress in that regard. She also kept a detailed chronology, including the times she phoned Laura to clarify or discuss or share an idea. Mary also willingly spent a day at the request of the researcher writing out the chronology of her action research as well as a narrative that was used as the basis for the case study presented here.

Lessons Learned

Mary and Laura's story strongly demonstrates that change in an educational setting can be a slow and long process and that educational leaders often find it difficult to continue working systematically towards their goals over an extended period of time. The outside assistance provided through coaching helps them maintain the momentum.

The time that Mary took to document what she did and when, and the assistance that Laura gave her in this regard, highlight another important aspect of the action research process—writing up "the story" to share with other leaders. Usually, educational leaders are more interested in carrying out their next action, rather than writing about their last. In this way, much valuable leadership theory is lost. Leaders need to build time for writing into their action research plans.

University partnerships, usually in the form of a researcher, alongside a programme of coaching, also assist leaders to write about their theory development. Such collaborative action research between researchers and educational institutions is vital for job-embedded development. Leaders' job conditions are often inimical to in-depth reflection on practice and, in turn, committed actions of praxis. Coaching and research collaborations help educational leaders overcome this barrier.

SUMMARY OF MAIN POINTS

Action research is:

- A natural outcome of an effective coaching process.
- An important theoretical framework for the change process.
- Effective for personal, professional, and institutional development.
- An intervention into daily leadership practice.
- Participatory, self-evaluative, site based, and concerns based.
- A tool to maintain a focus on improvement goals.
- Collaborative and develops communities of learners.
- An effective structure within which leaders can move consistently towards goals set.

PART TWO:
PRACTICE

Getting underway

CHAPTER OVERVIEW

Establishing and maintaining the coaching process is not without problems. In most situations, it is difficult for leaders not only to initiate the process on their own but also to sustain the relationship due to the busyness and intensification of their everyday work. This chapter outlines the processes important in developing the coaching partnership, including the selection of a partner, the regularity of contact, the development of trust and respect, building skills, and bringing commitment and stringency to the coaching process. The chapter also sets out the format for a first coaching session, outlines a typical coaching programme over a year, and aligns the coaching process with Fullan's (1985) model of the change process. The chapter concludes with a case study that documents how two principals developed a coaching relationship.

Developing the partnership

Selecting a coaching partner

The first step in initiating coaching between colleagues is determining who should partner whom. It is important that the leaders themselves have some say in who their coaching partner will be; that person should not be arbitrarily allocated. However, it is not always easy to find a suitable coach. Impression management (i.e., management focused on maintaining a positive reputation) and competition between institutions and between leaders within institutions often mean that leaders consider colleagues in neighbouring institutions or departments to be unsuitable candidates. This, despite the fact that, as research studies have shown, coaching can actually improve relationships between leaders to the extent that collaboration and collegiality again prevail. Within an educational institution, lack of "choice" can also be an issue. Those leaders working with an outside facilitator to establish the coaching partnership (see Chapter 10) might suggest two or three people they consider appropriate and then leave the facilitator to make the necessary approaches.

During the leadership coaching research, leaders often commented that they thought the coaching relationship most benefited them when they could work with leaders from institutions or departments of a similar size and type to their own, or from similar positions within an institution. The findings from the research confirmed that this was, indeed, the case. It does not matter if the two partners in the coaching relationship hold disparate goals and visions, or that their education communities are quite different, as long as the leaders feel able to relate fully to the experiences of their coaching partner. When this is the case, leaders are able to ask questions of one another that are appropriate for assisting reflection on leadership. As one leader said, "Similar size means facing similar sorts of problems."

Facilitating trust, respect, and confidentiality

Selection of coaching partners must be based on honesty and a respect for difference in leadership styles. Leaders willing to debate ideas and listen carefully to their partner make valuable coaches, as this leader attested:

> An open and receptive mind is important. Not a wholesale acceptance of
> anything and everything, but a willingness to consider multiple options and

ideas. Sound self-esteem is helpful in this as in all aspects of life. Honesty, reciprocal trust and respect are essential. Philosophical similarity is not paramount, in my view.

Trust is as vital in relation to those facilitating the coaching process as it is for the coaching partners themselves. But for all parties to the process, trust takes time to develop, and this time must be allowed for during the initiation phase of the partnership development. At first, the partners will be tentative, testing the extent to which they can trust one another, but, with time, they will become more and more open with each other in direct relation to the degree of trust engendered. Confidentiality of information shared is paramount to the developing trust, and a coach's personal integrity and professional ethics must be the ultimate guide here.

"That confidentiality is so important. We share a lot of things. He knows I wouldn't tell … anything. It is a privileged position, and you can never betray that trust, and you have to know that."

Leaders often fear that being too open with a coaching partner will lead to a lack of respect, especially if they conduct the operations in their institutions in quite different ways. One leader, early in one research study, said after his first shadow visit with his coach that he was concerned the relationship would not develop successfully because his coach did not seem to respect the way he did things in his institution:

> I found [coach] difficult to understand at times and was a little concerned that during his time to discuss things with me he seemed to be a little judgemental about what we discussed. I feel a bit apprehensive about the partnership at this stage.

It is therefore important that coaches are not judgemental about their partner's practice, but rather assume the role of critical friend in the reflection process.

Agreeing on regularity of contact

Regular contact at the beginning of the coaching relationship enhances the development of a rapport between the partners. The coaching research indicates that four- to six-weekly intervals between coaching sessions are viable, depending on the specificity or intensity of the particular project or issue under focus, and that a two- to three-hour session is more beneficial than one hour. The longer the period of time between meetings, the more likely it is that the two colleagues will lose the continuity and the more difficult they will find it to build the intimacy necessary to engage in open dialogue about the issues facing them in their institutions. Irregular contact also lessens the "conscience-based" imperative of coaching that ensures the systematic carrying out of action plans and monitoring of goals set. And, of course, coaching that becomes little more than a "one-off" visit can never be as professionally fulfilling as coaching that involves regular visits.

Another reason why regular contact is important is that partners accrue greater benefit from the coaching relationship when they work together regularly over a sustained period of time (Barnett, 1990; Robertson, 1995). As the research studies showed, leaders tended not to experience or realise the full benefits of the coaching until they had worked together for approximately one year. A further point relating to regularity of contact over time is that coaching is then more likely to become institutionalised into the partners' daily practice (Robertson, 1995).

Making a commitment

The many demands on leaders' time mean that the processes of coaching can easily be superseded by other events. To prevent this happening, those participating in coaching must be firmly committed to their own professional development. It is, as one leader stressed, a matter of priority and commitment: "Time! It is important to see the coaching as a vital part of professional development and make time for it."

"Time factors [are the greatest barrier]—fitting in times to visit/be visited, balancing this with all the other aspects of the day/ job. Realising the importance and benefits of visits has made it easier to prioritise these times."

When the leaders are as committed as each other to establishing and building a professional partnership, a coaching relationship is more likely to succeed. When coaching partners are not equally committed to the coaching process, and when they do not plan ahead by scheduling in, at an early stage, the times at which they will meet with one another over a year or so, disappointment and disillusionment are the outcomes.

Exercising stringency

The small amount of time that leaders generally have available for their own leadership development (including through coaching) means that they must make the most of that time. Leaders must agree in advance to conduct their meetings with one another with stringency. They also need to agree in advance to bring a formal, structured approach to each meeting, to interview each other, and to record descriptive accounts of behaviours during observations. Without this degree of formality or stringency, leaders are likely to lapse into general conversation that, while possibly providing each other with support, is likely to offer very little in the way of challenge.

Building skills

No simple formula can guarantee the success of the coaching process, but spending time getting the basics right during its early stage does appear to have a marked effect on whether the coaching develops into a relationship where the partners are equally committed to each other's ongoing leadership development. However, getting the basics right is one thing. The other is ensuring that leaders build into their sessions, across the period of coaching, an opportunity to practise and extend those early attributes, skills, and procedures so they can participate ever more effectively in their leadership development. This is where the outside facilitator is particularly useful. This person's knowledge of the processes of coaching and the theory of leadership helps leaders determine what they need to do and know in this regard, and how to go about achieving these aims.

The more leaders work together, the more skills they will develop, and the more they will be able to work in different ways with their coaches. The skills for effective coaching are:

- listening;
- reflective interviewing;
- self-assessment;
- goal setting;
- developing action plans;
- setting time frames;
- observing and describing practice;
- giving effective feedback; and
- acquiring knowledge of the action research process.

These skills, described in detail in the next two chapters, help leaders develop new ways of thinking about learning. They are predicated on the principle of the importance of reflection, firstly for self-awareness and, ultimately, for self-efficacy and agency brought about by a greater understanding of the leadership role and the social and political influences on education. These skills lead coaches through dialogue towards praxis, and are thus an intentional bridge between theory and practice.

Setting up a coaching folder

Reflection is aided by keeping records of the coaching process. Early in the relationship, coaching partners need to determine what type of records will be kept and who will keep them. A chronology of times spent together and outcomes of sessions provides one important set of records, as do self-assessment, goal-setting, and action plans. These sets of materials should all be carefully filed for future reference. Some form of reflection, either field notes or a short reflective statement written during or immediately after each session, can also benefit the ongoing leadership development. The reflective exercises in the next chapter can also be kept in the coaching folder and referred to over time.

The coaching sessions

The getting started considerations just outlined form part of the content of the first meetings between the partners. From there, partners can ease themselves into the skills and procedures of coaching by setting up sessions that follow the steps below. (These are presented at this time in summary form only; greater detail of skill development is given in Chapters 7 and 8.)

Throughout the entire process, coaches need to keep in mind these points:

- The process takes time to work.
- The process should never be hurried.
- Every encounter is valuable.
- Each partner will at times be the coach, at other times the coached.
- Just as good leaders know how to lead and to follow, good coaches know how to coach and be coached.

First sessions

1. Complete a coaching development workshop to practise skills of active listening and reflective interviewing (see Chapter 7).

2. Browse through this book again to ensure familiarity with the principles and processes of coaching.
3. Confirm the date for a first interview meeting. (Ideally, as noted above, partners will have set out meeting dates during their very earliest meetings.)
4. Meet in Partner A's context (whether institution, classroom, or office) to carry out a context and/or self-assessment interview (see Chapter 7), make notes, and confirm the date of the next meeting.
5. Meet in Partner B's context, carry out a context and/or self-assessment interview, make notes, and confirm plans for a shadow (observation) visit.

Subsequent sessions

1. Complete a coaching development workshop to revisit the skills of observing and describing practice, self-assessment, and goal setting.
2. Confirm the date for Partner B to do a shadow observation of Partner A.
3. Carry out the observation. This should not be too formal; the idea is just to let it flow.
4. Carry out a reflective interview and goal setting as soon as possible after the observation.
5. Confirm plans for Partner A to do a shadow observation of Partner B (if reciprocal coaching).
6. Carry out a reflective interview and goal setting as soon as possible after the observation.

Further sessions

1. Complete a coaching development workshop to practise the skill of giving evaluative feedback.
2. Include feedback and all other skills in future sessions as necessary.

A typical session

An acronym often used in coaching books to guide the format of coaching meetings is GROW (Eaton & Johnson, 2001; Landsberg, 2003; Whitmore, 2002). G stands for Goal. R stands for Reality. O stands for Options. As for W, Eaton and Johnson use WHEN, Whitmore uses WHAT (will you do?), and Landsberg uses WRAP-UP. The latter, "wrap-up", is perhaps the most useful expression, as it can incorporate the when and the what, as in, "What will you do from here on in?" "When shall we have our next meeting?"

However, before following through with the steps dictated by the acronym, the coaching partners can "warm up" by having the person assuming the role of coach ask the coached partner such questions as:

- What's been happening since my last visit with you?
- What have you learned from some of the leadership actions and incidents?
- What have you been thinking about lately?

The coach must remember to listen *actively* to the answers, to what is said and not said, and to follow up with questions accordingly. At any one session, one person takes the role of coach throughout. If this is a reciprocal coaching relationship, the partner assumes the role of coach in the leader's own context during the next session.

From here, the partners follow through with reflective interviewing and self-assessment in a professional goal-setting session structured by the acronyms GROW and SMART (Eaton & Johnson, 2001; Landsberg, 2003), (see the chart on the next page).

The developing relationship

The coaching relationship that develops over time represents a process of change in leaders' professional ways of working. Leaders therefore need to understand how this process works, not only in terms of actual coaching processes but also in terms of developing the coaching relationship.

Fullan's (1985) model of the change process is particularly useful in this regard, because it easily describes the development stages of any successful coaching relationship and, indeed, any change process. Fullan holds that all change involves an initiation phase followed by an implementation phase. If the implementation phase is successful, this leads to an institutionalisation phase, where new ways of working become embedded in the culture of an organisation.

During the *initiation phase* of the coaching relationship, time must be allowed for trust and confidence to develop. There is no rush to move

- **GOAL**—Review the major goals set at previous meeting(s) and discuss the focus for this visit.

  Questions to ask (**Specific, Measured**): What progress have you made towards your goals? What will you be doing when you have achieved the goal? What will it look like? How will you measure achievement of the goal? What would you like to achieve from this session?
- **REALITY**—The partners together discuss and examine contextual issues around the achievement or non-achievement of goals and the situation as it currently is. The coach endeavours to ask further questions of the partner that relate directly to and elicit further reflection on these considerations.

  Questions to ask (**Achievable**): What has worked in previous similar situations? What might hinder you in this process? What was the outcome from what you have already done? What issues were there? What resources can you call on? What was successful in moving you towards your goal(s)? What is the current state of play? What is worrying you most?
- **OPTIONS**—The partners decide, as an outcome of their discussion and reflection, on the options the coached leader could take regarding his or her goals. At this stage, the partners need to explore every possibility, to think laterally and outside the square. And this is where the coach is particularly valuable in terms of providing outside challenges to the partner's thinking and offering suggestions.

  Questions to ask (**Relevant**): What options are available? What would [someone else] think to do in this situation? What is the most outlandish thing you can think of to do? What will work against these options being successful? What will facilitate your progress? What would you specifically like feedback on?
- **WRAP-UP**—Discuss which actions will follow from here, based on a selection from the options generated above. Set goals and confirm the time of the next session.

  Questions to ask (**Time**): When do you think you will achieve this goal? What will be your first step, and when? Is there any support the coach or a consultant could give in this process? When will you meet to review progress?

Note: If the meeting between the two partners involves a shadow observation, then the coach needs to include the following steps in the goal-setting session described above:
- Observe the action.
- Take careful, descriptive notes.
- Select one incident for reflective interview.
- Take 5 to 10 minutes alone for assessment and reflection:
  - Fill in notes from observation.
  - Prepare questions for reflective interview.
- Resume meeting with partner.
- Describe the leadership actions observed.
- Carry out the reflective interview.
- Give feedback.

into observation of practice at this stage. Leaders should be given as many opportunities as possible to talk about their practice, their values, and beliefs, and what they are trying to achieve. They need to understand each other's role and the context for the leadership practice under scrutiny. They also need to learn what is important to their partner and that person's practice. The coach must keep this in mind as she or he facilitates the process with the leader. If an outside facilitator or consultant is working with pairs of leaders to develop the peer coaching relationships, it is important that they, too, demonstrate integrity to the process by recognising the importance of process and relationship versus task achievement.

The *implementation phase* begins when leaders are comfortable enough to focus on deeper educational issues and are open to new ideas and ways of working. They will bring a more formal focus to their meetings, be ready to observe each other in practice, and will be able to give and receive constructive evaluative feedback on their leadership. The facilitator's critique of and feedback about the developing coaching relationship (shadowing the leaders as they coach in their institutions or classrooms) are invaluable at this stage. The leaders begin to recognise the leadership strengths they both bring to the coaching partnership and to utilise these more fully in the developing relationship. They will start to act as consultant to each other.

"Formal structured interviews have to be planned for. That is the only way, because otherwise you don't let it happen... . [You have to say,] 'We will start our interview now.' ... [T]hey are very worthwhile."

In the *institutionalisation phase*, leaders become more autonomous and authoritative in their coaching relationship. Their reliance on the input of the outside facilitator (if they have used one) to sustain the process lessens, and they will have a sound appreciation of how coaching practices support their continuing leadership development, which they will initiate themselves. The leaders may be prepared at this stage to take on a new partner or partners in the process. They may wish to teach other leaders the skills of coaching and to work as an outside facilitator with these people in order to widen the developing community of learners, or build leadership capacity in their institutions. The point at which coaching practices become an accepted and integrated way of working in these leaders' institutions is the point at which the practices have become institutionalised.

EXAMPLE OF A YEAR'S COACHING PROGRAMME

February
- The first professional development coaching skills workshop
- Followed by context interview in each partner's leadership context

March
- The first shadow observation in Context A
- Followed by a reflective interview and goal setting

April
- The first shadow observation in Context B
- Followed by a reflective interview and goal setting

April
- Meet with other coaches in workshop for ideas, debriefing and further skill development

May
- The second shadow observation in Context A, with related feedback and goal setting
- Action planning and self-assessment

June
- The second shadow observation in Context B, with related feedback and goal setting

August—October
- Implementation of action plans with coaching support as negotiated

October
- The third shadow observation in Context A, with related feedback and goal setting
- The third shadow observation in Context B, with related feedback and goal setting

November
- Reviewing the year
- Reviewing goals
- Resetting goals

Note: If the coaching is integrated with the performance management systems in the institution, the formal appraisal interview may be conducted and recorded during the November session. Also, while three shadow observations/reflective interviews a year for each person is minimal, this number is perhaps realistic given the demands on leaders of their educational contexts. With vicarious learning through reflection on another's practice, in a reciprocal coaching process, each partner would then be involved in six coaching sessions focused on leadership practice during the year.

CASE STUDY: Snapshots of a developing relationship

The story below traces the coaching relationship that developed between Sue and Rawiri, an experienced principal and a first-time principal respectively, who participated in the leadership research. It is set out according to Fullan's (1985) model, and is told mainly through Sue's and Rawiri's voices, and through quotes taken out of guided written reflections or the transcripts of interviews conducted throughout the two years of research. My field notes and other comments (in italics) provide the linking narrative.

INITIATION: First six months
Establishing the partnership

First meeting

Sue: Although we are in the same district and teach within three kilometres of each other, our schools are quite different. Although we have differing visions and priorities, the end result is the same—to provide the best possible educational outcomes for our children.

Rawiri: We talked for another two hours after you [the facilitator] had left, and we found it extremely valuable. We have set a future shadowing date in each other's schools and look positively towards working together in the research.

First professional development meeting: Moving through lack of surety

9 A.M.

Rawiri: I arrived with things on my mind—the community worker at school; the employment service worker starting next term; transport for tomorrow's trip; forgot my [cassette] tape [for researcher].

Sue: I am not yet fully clear about this partnership. My expectations are developing as we go along.

3 P.M.

Sue: [We've been] getting to know each other's communities and problems and realising that perhaps problems weren't as great as originally thought.

Good to hear different approaches to same or similar jobs, and important to have a partner with same or similar needs.

Rawiri: I feel I have a little more idea of what I am supposed to be doing. I am lucky to have Sue as my partner. I feel very comfortable with her, and I am sure it won't be long before we will share almost anything.

Sue: We have set some objectives and times [to meet] and are happy to continue with the partnership. Personally, I am much clearer about where we go from here.

IMPLEMENTATION: Second six months
Developing and maintaining the partnership

Sue: Rawiri and I have been slow to get our shadowing done this term because of other commitments. I know we are meant to prioritise these tasks, but the following is a typical example of what happens to teaching principals. Just as I was leaving school at 3 p.m. a distressed? concerned? parent arrived determined to see one of my teachers. My teacher requested that I stay for the interview.

The shadowing that Sue referred to was a staff meeting being conducted by Rawiri. Sue did eventually attend a staff meeting that Rawiri was leading so that she could observe and provide feedback on how he worked with his staff. She described her first experience of shadow coaching as follows.

Sue: It was interesting to hear another principal promoting visions, policies, positive attitudes, and involvement to a staff who, like all staff, have individual and varying attitudes. I came away deciding that, as principals, we have to be constantly motivating children, staff, and communities.

Goal-setting session

Sue: GOAL: to set a better system of appraisal in place. ... [Rawiri can help me with this by being] able to first observe and then assist me in getting *all* staff on board. [This session] made me consider carefully preferred outcomes.

Rawiri: Kia ora. I've just come out of a really stressful period from about the last five or six weeks—school, and union, and principals—it has been a really hard time, and it has placed pressure on my family. I notice that a lot of smaller things upset me that normally I wouldn't worry about. It really does affect your home life. So I have just got my head above water—just this week—and now I feel really tired—I am looking forward to just keeping the school running—just doing the day-to-day things. ... I was just thinking about board of trustee meetings and writing the report and how stressful it can be prior to a board of trustees meeting—basically, because you never know what is going to hit you when you get there.

Sue: I think you have to come to terms with the fact that you are going to make mistakes, but the important thing is not repeating those mistakes.

Rawiri: I find that I am not always sure when I have made mistakes 'cause I haven't had the kickback yet. So I tell people when they ask, that 'Things seem to be going all right,' but I am waiting for the letter to say, 'Why haven't you done this?' ... It will probably come quite a long while after. ... [My goal is] to lead my staff into the area of data gathering in a non-threatening way, to delegate jobs to the board of trustees and not do them all myself. [Sue's role as coach will be] to monitor my progress; share her first steps in this area.

Sue and Rawiri then went on, in this coaching session that I was observing, to talk further about their boards of trustees. Sue had worked hard to get hers to take far more responsibility and was pleased with the amount of work they had carried out. Sue shared with Rawiri the view that the members of her board should take responsibility for their portfolios and get the work done. Rawiri said he had to do most of the work and that his board looked to him for all the answers, which he was finding a huge responsibility. The two compared how their boards operated, and Rawiri agreed to shadow observe Sue at her next board meeting.

Meeting after the shadow observation

Rawiri: I really admired you, Sue, when you told them that about the health issue. In my [board] meetings from then on, I just kept writing down that they were responsible, until one day there was a near accident, and I was able to say, 'You guys are responsible for this.' That really helped me.

Sue and Rawiri's discussion then turned to the amount of money budgeted for the curriculum and the deferred maintenance in their schools.

Rawiri: One thing that really scares me is that you can go and get $16,000 to reseal the tennis court, and if you tried to get $16,000 to put into science, you wouldn't get it! ... I want to have a staff meeting on this next week—just to get the wheels rolling before next term. I am quite excited about it actually.

Sue: I remember being so taken aback when one of the staff members questioned me on measurement and evaluation. I was so fired up, I just imagined that everyone else would be too.

Rawiri: I have thought about that, too, and thought about a couple of questions I could ask them (they may be the wrong questions), but I know I could say, 'You know Johnny Smith, what year is he reading at?' and I know that would pull the rugs from right under their feet and the defences would come up straight away, and it wouldn't work, so I have really been trying to think about this.

Sue: You will find that the enthusiastic ones will help to bring on the other ones because they will start bringing things of theirs and say, 'Look at this,' and things get left lying around and others pick them up.

Rawiri: The enormity of the task has just come home. The quality of the school and where it is all at is right here in the classrooms where the work is done. It is hard work. So I expect I have just answered my own question, then, that I have to lead the way by lifting my own standards. By doing that, I can actually begin to raise theirs.

INSTITUTIONALISATION: Second year
Reflecting on the coaching

Rawiri: I have found a principal that I can confide in. I trust her and enjoy listening to her views. And, yes, I do enjoy working with her. Problems? Sometimes we talk too much. We need to set an action-research plan.

Sue: I think these things take time to make them work. I needed the year before I could see how valuable working like this with a colleague could be. We got to know each other and what we wanted to achieve. I think, then, that after an interview you could come in and keep going back to our objectives, rather than just chatting, which we did quite well ... we have had time to develop respect and trust. I didn't know Rawiri very well until this. I had just met him.

Rawiri: I sort of take this for granted now really. Like I said, it would be a shame if we didn't have our [coaching] partnership.

Advice to others starting out ...

Rawiri: Find a partnership that suits your style. It helps if you are not in competition with one another. If the first [partner] doesn't work, at least try one other. Have some open talking sessions about whatever comes up. This is more difficult ... make formal sessions to observe and reflect on them. If you are a teaching principal and, depending on the success of the partnership, you may or may not meet regularly out of school. Two heads can be better than one.

Sue: Developing a partnership has proved to be a very supportive way of working professionally with another leader ... my present partnership will continue, as I believe we have both found it to our advantage.

SUMMARY OF MAIN POINTS

To develop successfully, coaching relationships need:

- trust, confidentiality and respect;
- a commitment to ongoing professional development;
- time to develop effectively;
- regularity of contact;
- ongoing practice in and building of coaching skills;
- sessions conducted with stringency (i.e., with structure and purpose);
- initiation, implementation, and institutionalisation phases; and
- a consideration of each leader's unique needs.

Coaching the skills
that build trust and
understanding

CHAPTER OVERVIEW

It is most important that any coaching partnership maintains the principle that, first and foremost, coaches are effective learners and enter the coaching relationship willing to learn. To be effective, coaches need to be equipped with specific skills. This chapter looks at the skills required for the initiation phase of coaching, where the main emphasis is on building trust and understanding between the partners in an unhurried manner. The skills of listening and reflective interviewing are outlined and then followed by a description of the skills of the context interview. This important interview is conducted during a visit to the partner's workplace to observe the realities of the day-to-day leadership practice for that person. The descriptions of each of the skills are complemented by activities that the reader can work through individually or with a coach, in a workshop session.

Active listening

Active listening is one of the most important of the coaching skills and is one of the first requirements of effective dialogue (Isaacs, 1999). To listen for even three or four minutes without interrupting and without sharing one's own stories or giving advice is something that leaders often find difficult. Within the coaching relationship, active listening gives each leader, in turn, the freedom to articulate their practice, to justify why they are doing what they are doing, and to reflect on the impact they believe their actions have. On first being given the opportunity to speak uninterrupted, leaders often comment on how seldom this happens and of how strange, yet liberating, it feels. Leaders also talk about the effect that this one small skill development session has on their everyday work. They find themselves "listening first, in order to learn" (Covey, 1989) and not interrupting others when they are telling their stories. Suspension of judgement is also an important aspect of dialogue that involves active listening (Isaacs, 1999).

Listening guidelines and process

To be active listeners, coaches should:

- give the speaker full attention;
- encourage that person to keep talking;
- not break into conversation by sharing "war stories" or their own experience;
- not give advice;
- take careful note of what is said, in writing if necessary;
- not ask questions;
- focus in particular on what is said about leadership practice; and
- listen as well for what is *not* said and for what is important to the speaker.

Activities to build the skill

The following are short reflective activities that give leaders opportunities to talk about their practice and give their coach opportunities to practise actively listening. The activities can be structured into workshops or used by readers to reflect individually on their leadership as they read this book and in preparation for working with a coach in the future.

Reflective activity 1

A) On a sheet of paper, write down three leadership situations that you have been involved in recently and that have involved other people. Such situations might include a departmental meeting or senior management team meeting, strategic planning sessions, talking with parents about the placement of their child, speaking with an incompetent staff member, or working on induction with new staff. They might be positive events, or involve issues that have been worrying you.

B) Now put an asterisk (*) by the situation that you would find valuable to talk about in a coaching situation.

C) Share this situation with your coach, telling them as much as you can about the situation, what happened, what you were thinking about then and are thinking about now, the issues you face, what might happen from here on—in fact, anything that comes to mind. Spend three to four minutes doing this, during which time your coach will be required to actively listen to you.

D) Take time with your partner to reflect on the listening process. What was the experience as the listener? What was it like for the speaker? What were the mental processes occurring as you were listening/speaking?

E) Repeat the activity, with a different issue, again focusing on the reflective processes.

Extension: Your leadership is in the multitude of tasks and actions that you perform each day—even if you feel at the end of a day that you have not "done anything". Talk about, analyse, and reflect on some of the things you do in your daily practice.

Reflective activity 2

What are three things important to you in your leadership practice? If your coach came and shadowed you for a week, what might be some of the things that you would be seen to do on a regular basis? For example, are you visible in the institution? Do you hold your meetings in different venues? Do you analyse data to provide evidence at meetings for future action?

A) Write down three things of importance and then jot down why you do them and what impact you think they have on the quality of learning in your institution.

B) For each item, write your answers under these headings:
  - What I do.
  - Why I do it.
  - Impact on learning.

Extension: Take your listed items and consider them according to this schema (after Smyth, 1989):

What do I do?	(Describe)
What does this mean?	(Inform)
How did I come to be like this?	(Construct)
How might I do things differently?	(Reconstruct)

Reflective activity 3

This activity requires you to think about the values and beliefs that form your educational platform, which in turn underpin the decisions that you make. Would others you work with be able to articulate your educational platform? Do the people you work with know what is important to you and why? In other words, do you "speak the language of educational leadership" in your work?

A) Take the situations and items you listed in Activities 1 and 2, and think about them in relation to these questions:
  - Which of your values and beliefs about education do these relate to?
  - How do you believe these values and beliefs make a difference to the quality of learning offered in your institution?
  - What have you identified about your values and beliefs?

B) Now consider what you deem particularly important in terms of education?
  - How does your viewpoint affect the decisions you make?
  - How does it affect the way you work with others in setting your institutional goals?

Reflective activity 4

Your educational platform is the "soapbox" you stand on when you make a decision about educational issues. This activity follows on from Activity 3 in that it allows you to identify most exactly your educational platform and then to use this in another active listening session with your coaching partner (Activity 5).

A) Copy and then fill out the questionnaire (adapted from work by Sergiovanni & Starratt, 1979, 2002) on the next pages. Work right through the questionnaire without stopping. In other words, write down what immediately comes into your head. You will have a chance to revisit what you have written later on.

B) Work through this identification process on your own.

C) When you have done that, take your answers from those sections of the questionnaire that you believe have particular significance for your own work and reflect on each independently. If you are in a workshop situation, you can listen to how other educational leaders responded to each aspect of the platform. If you wish to add anything to your answers as a result of your reflection, place this in the "Afterthoughts" sections.

Reflective activity 5

A) After you have worked right through the platform, share your ideas with your coach or other leaders. There should be no debate or discussion, just active listening. Add any more ideas you gain as a result of this activity in the "Afterthoughts". When you have completed all commentary on the educational platforms to your satisfaction, open up the session to questioning and discussion. There is no need to try to reach consensus. The most important thing is to understand why people believe the things they do and how this informs their leadership practice.

B) At this point you should also be able to identify your own "pedagogy of leadership practice", that is, what you believe to be important in the *way* that you work with people. Do you believe in, for example:
   - consultation;
   - pastoral care of colleagues;
   - learning communities;
   - new ideas and innovation;
   - risk taking;
   - shared decision making;
   - developing leadership in others?

Make your own list, and then talk with your partner/coach about what each item means in terms of your work.

QUESTIONNAIRE

1. Aims of Education

- If you had to give one overall general aim of education, what would it be?

- Extrapolating from that, what, in order of priority, are the three most important aims of education for the students in your institution?

- Afterthoughts?

2. View of Knowledge

- What is knowledge? How do people become "knowledgeable"? What does it mean to be knowledgeable?

- Afterthoughts?

3. Major Achievements

- What are your major achievements over the past year, particularly as they relate to your students' achievement or colleagues' work? List those that relate specifically to your work.

- Afterthoughts?

4. Social Significance of What Students Learn

– What do you think this is?

– Afterthoughts?

5. Image of the Learner

– What are your assumptions about how one learns? How do you view the learner?

– Afterthoughts?

6. Image of the Curriculum

– What are your attitudes about the value of the curriculum or programmes offered?

– Afterthoughts?

7. Image of the Teacher

– What is your view about the role of the teacher?

– Afterthoughts?

8. Pedagogy

– What is your preferred mode of teaching and learning (and/or leadership)?

– Afterthoughts?

9. Language Used in Learning Situations

– Describe the type of language you use when working with groups.

– Can you give any examples of actual phrases you hear yourself saying?

– Afterthoughts?

10. Teacher–Student and Working Relationships

– What is your preferred type of teacher–student relationship?

– What is your preferred type of relationship when working with colleagues, parents, board of trustee members, etc?

– Afterthoughts?

11. Institutional Climate

– What are the three most important qualities, norms, or values for you in a workplace?

– Afterthoughts?

12. Image of Parents and/or Community Consultation

– What is your image of the "place" and role of parents and/or community consultation in education?

– Afterthoughts?

13. Purpose of Monitoring Quality of Teaching and Learning

– What do you think the purpose or goal is of quality assurance in educational institutions? Whose role is it?

– Afterthoughts?

14. Process of Monitoring Teaching and Learning

– What method of monitoring teaching and learning do you prefer for your institution? What works best?

– Afterthoughts?

15. Quality of Instruction in Your Institution

– What do your consider is your role in influencing the quality of instruction and programmes in your institution?

– Afterthoughts?

Reflective interviewing

Questioning partners in a way that encourages them to critically reflect on their leadership practice is the essential skill of coaching, and is the one that leaders are most likely to have to learn and practise over a reasonable period of time. This technique provides opportunities for those being questioned to explore their knowledge, skills, experiences, attitudes, beliefs, and values (Lee, 1993), and it leaves ownership of the reflection, and any judgement arising out of it, in their hands. It is important that leaders do not feel coaching involves a colleague coming in and telling them how to lead their school or department or institution or centre, but rather that this person is someone who will help facilitate an understanding of their practice. Such an approach is more powerful than telling or giving advice because it is empowering. The person being asked the questions must come up with answers that will work for them and their particular context, because doing this facilitates ownership of the outcomes and process of change. A telling or controlling approach leads to either dependency or resistance, neither of which is conducive to rich professional development.

There should be no rush to move onto other coaching-related skills until reflective interviewing has become a comfortable, established skill. As leaders look back on their developing coaching relationship, it is likely that they will recognise that their ability to dialogue about their leadership practice is commensurate with their ability to employ the skill of reflective interviewing.

Question levels

There are at least three types or levels of questions that leaders can use to assist their coaching partner reflect critically on their practice. These are based on those formulated by Lee (1993) and Lee and Barnett (1994). For an example of how these three levels work within the context of a reflective interview, see the example on the next page.

Level 1

Level 1 questions are designed to clarify thinking about events, situations, actions, and feelings. Such questions often start with: "Tell me ... what, when, if, whether, who, how and why?" They are used to make sure that leaders in the coaching role have all the necessary information about an observation they have just made or are quite clear about the details of an incident that their partner has just described. Examples might be: "Tell me how often you have these meetings?" "Who sets the agenda?" "How many members attend the planning meetings?"

Level 2

These are used to clarify purpose, reasons, and intended consequences. They often start with how, why, who, which, and are concerned with probing the reasons as to why a leader has taken a particular action and what that person sees as the intended outcomes of that action. Examples include: "What is the purpose of these meetings?" "What do you hope will develop from them?" "How do (or will) they affect learning and teaching?"

Level 3

This third level of questions should move leaders into exploring the basis or outcomes of their actions. These "linking" questions are often called "So what/how …?" questions. Examples are: "So what will happen next?" "So what might you do differently?" "So what impact will this have on the culture of this institution?" "So how does this link with your goal of shared decision making?" "So how does this support your improvement plan?" "So how does this lead towards achieving your vision?" "So how does this relate to your profile document?"

Reflective interviewing guidelines and process

Coaches need to follow quite specific guidelines when conducting reflective interviews. They also need to consider afterwards how effective the interview sessions were in stimulating their coaching partner to think critically about their leadership practice.

To encourage critical reflection:

- Base questions on the experiences of the respondent (not "What if …" situations).
- Use non-judgemental wording.
- Maintain a neutral tone of voice.
- Be prepared to follow up initial questions but note down a few questions at each of the three question levels before starting the interview.

The coach in the following scenario has employed the three levels of questioning, with the aim of facilitating in-depth reflection on the part of her partner.

COMMENT: This morning I observed you carrying out a strategic planning session.

Level 1 Questions
- How often do you carry these out?
- Who is usually present?
- What are the goals of the institution?
- How were they developed?

Level 2 Questions
- Why did you carry out this session at this point of time?
- How did you structure your session? Why did you structure it this way?
- What is the purpose or goal of the strategic planning sessions? Why?
- How will you know you have achieved the goal?
- What might facilitate progress towards your institutional goals?
- What may hinder your progress?
- Why do you believe these sessions are important?
- What do you think are the most important benefits for those concerned? For the institution?

Level 3 Questions
- How do you believe this strategic planning session will impact on learning and teaching and the programmes in this institution in the future?
- How do these meetings assist you in your work as a senior leader in this institution?
- So what effect do these sessions have on your overall leadership development programme?
- How does this link with the overall vision for the institution?
- So what would you do differently next time you run such a session?
- What specifically helped you move towards achieving your goals?

- Use active listening skills, such as nodding, looking at the person, perhaps using a short question prompt like, "What happened then?" Do not break into the flow of talk or ask questions that might change the speaker's direction of focus.
- Refrain from giving advice disguised as questions.
- Do not break into general dialogue until the interview is officially over.

The opportunity to practise reflective interviewing must be an integral part of the coaching process. Time must also be set aside for leaders to discuss with their coaches their experiences of the *process*, so that they can use the insights gained to develop advanced reflective interviewing techniques.

After an observation or active listening session, leaders in the coaching role should take five to 10 minutes to note down some questions—perhaps two at each level—that they could ask their partner about this leadership incident. However, the number of questions asked should be kept as low as possible. It is not a game of 20 questions; the aim for coaches is to listen actively. Their partners know the rules and how to play the game (good coaches make their processes overt), so will probably start off and work through the answers to many of the questions listed before their coach has a chance to ask them!

An activity to build the skill

Reflective activity 6

A) Take the leadership situation you described in Reflective Activity 1.
B) Revisit it now in light of the three levels of questions. Tell your coach what your intended outcome was and how it relates to, or has impacted on, your leadership in your institution.
C) Follow through with an active listening session, in which your coach should also employ careful questioning, using the three different levels, to help you critically reflect on your leadership practice and goals for your institution.
D) A prompt that your coach might employ here is: "Think back to the leadership experience that you were just interviewed about. In light of the reflective questioning and discussion, and in relation to a similar future incident, consider these questions:
  - What would you do differently?
  - What would you do the same?

- Did the reflective interviewing highlight anything for you?
- Was the reflective interviewing useful?
- In what ways?
- How could the reflective interviewing be improved?"

Context interviewing

The context interview is generally the first field-based reflective interview that the leaders carry out with their coaches. This interview is most effective when the partners have practised the skills of active listening and reflective interviewing in a workshop coaching situation. The interview is called a context interview because it refers to the context(s) in which the leader works, whether the classroom, the department, the office and/or the meeting-room. The observation should involve a type of "show and tell" session, in which coaches can look at their partner's rooms, resources, displays, files, and programmes, and perhaps meet other staff with whom the leader works.

The aim of this exercise is for coaches to become thoroughly familiar with the context in which their partners conduct their actions. This degree of familiarity is important and should not be assumed prior to the observation, even if the partners feel they know each other's context. The way individual leaders perceive their context is unique to their leadership, because each leader's values, beliefs and experiences are unique.

"There is definitely a challenge and there is work involved, but it is rewarding and it's very worthwhile."

The basis of the context interview employed in the coaching model is the first part of the Leadership Framework (see Table 2), adapted from Bossert, Dwyer, Rowan, and Lee (1982). This first section of the framework (Table 2) sets out the main areas and associated examples of topics to be covered during the interview, namely the institutional context, the educational community, the governing bodies, and the leader's own beliefs, and experiences. Table 3 outlines the content of the full framework.

Context interviewing guidelines and process

The interview is carried out on site relatively early in the coaching relationship and is linked directly to the leaders' reflection on the Leadership Framework. The context observation and interview should not be undertaken until the leaders being observed have had an opportunity for individual reflection

TABLE 2: ITEMS GUIDING THE CONTEXT INTERVIEW WITHIN THE CONTEXT OF THE LEADERSHIP FRAMEWORK

Institutional Context	Community	Governing Bodies	Beliefs and Experiences

• Regional
• National
• Professional affiliations
• Charter/Policies/ Codes
• Profile
• Staffing
  – Strengths
  – Experiences
  – Issues
	• Locale
	• Socioeconomic status
	• Ethnic composition and diversity
	• Expectations
	• Values
	• Transiency
	• Resources
	• Support
	• Internal/ external politics
		• Human resources
		• Ministry of Education
		• Review Office
		• Board
		• Associations
		• Committees
		• Religious bodies
		• Legislation
		• Tertiary Education Commission
			• Professional experiences
			• Personal history— education and social
			• Philosophy and vision
			• Cultural perspectives
			• Religious or spiritual influences

Note: Adapted from S. T. Bossert, D. C. Dwyer, B. Rowan, & G. V. Lee (1982), The instructional management role of the principal, *Educational Administration Quarterly, 18*, 34—64.

TABLE 3: THE FULL LEADERSHIP FRAMEWORK

Background/ Context	Leadership Activities	Resources	Instructional Organisation	Outcomes
• Institutional context • Community • Governance context • Beliefs and experiences	• Routine behaviours • Goal setting • Planned behaviours	• Instructional climate • Collegial relationships • Policy • Values • Institutional culture	• Curriculum delivery • Instructional programmes • Pedagogy • Student groupings • Assessment • Feedback and appraisal • Quality assurance	• Programmes • Professional practices • Achievement

Note: Adapted from S. T. Bossert, D. C. Dwyer, B. Rowan, & G. V. Lee, (1982), The instructional management role of the principal, *Educational Administration Quarterly, 18*, 34—64.

on the framework and a discussion with their coach on their educational platform (see Reflective Activity 4). It is important that the observation and subsequent interview help leaders become aware of how each and every leadership action impacts on their leadership framework.

The information that should be covered by the interview thus relates to leaders' own educational backgrounds, beliefs and philosophies, the political and social context influencing their leadership, the types of communities they are working in, and the particular aspects of their work that make their leadership unique. The context interview process itself is quite explicit and involves these steps.

A) *Leader being observed*
- Reflect on each of the four aspects of the Leadership Framework and how each affects your own leadership in the institution.
- Share your context information with your coach; walk around your areas of responsibility, showing and explaining what you do and why you do what you do.
- Use the notes you made prior to this session to describe yourself and your context to your coach. This now forms the basis of your *context interview*—the first in-depth discussion you will have with your coach/partner on site.

B) *Coach*
- Actively listen.
- Ask reflective questions to clarify or seek additional information.

Activities to build the skill
Reflective activity 7

A) On your own, rule a piece of paper into five columns, and head the columns with the headings of the Leadership Framework in Table 3 (Background/Context, Leadership Activities, Resources, Instructional Organisation, Outcomes).

B) Assign each of the following leadership items to their appropriate columns.
- There is a negative perception about the institution in the local community.
- Very little hard data are available on student enrolment and/or achievement.
- Ten percent of the budget is allocated for professional development.
- Teachers have designated reflection times built into work structures.

- Few incidences of (staff or student) bullying occur.
- Teachers meet regularly for dialogue about teaching.
- Institution receives funding from entrepreneurial contracts.
- Leaders observe teaching and give feedback.
- Half of the teaching staff are new to the institution. Veterans resist change.
- Leader talks to students personally.
- Innovation is part of the institutional culture.
- Teachers are involved in team teaching.
- Eighty percent of the budget is allocated to salary.
- Students are bilingual.
- Performance management systems involve all staff in appraisal annually.
- Teachers are involved in allocating students to learning groups and/ or classes.
- Students are interested in learning and enjoy their study.
- Portfolios are used for goal setting.
- Staff consistently research their own practice.
- Board members take a keen interest in institutional governance.

Reflective activity 8

A) With your answers to Activity 7 in hand, join with your coaching partner or a group of leaders to discuss your placement of the items.

B) When you have done this, use these questions to guide your reflection on the session.
   - What discussion occurred during the session?
   - How do these factors, designated to parts of the framework, influence educational leadership?
   - What influenced your decisions?

C) Look again at your sheet of answers, and identify two or three outcomes that you would like to achieve in your school/class/institution this year. Ask yourself these questions:
   - What are the context factors that would influence how well you achieve these goals?
   - What will be the restraining influences? How might you work around these?
   - What resources will facilitate you meeting your goals?

Reflective activity 9

This activity gives you the opportunity to reflect on the usefulness of the skills you have learned from this chapter. Ask these questions to guide your reflection.

- What has the reflection around your education context helped you identify in terms of your leadership practice?
- How has the coach's questioning assisted in the process of reflection?
- What part has listening played in terms of your ability to focus on and describe your leadership practice?

SUMMARY OF MAIN POINTS

- Initiating the coaching process and building trust and understanding about a leader's work take a variable amount of time depending on the leader's degree of familiarity with the coach, the degree of comfort with the process of critiquing his or her own practice, and his or her experience level. It also depends on the coach's skills.

- It is important not to rush the process but to assess when the time is appropriate to move the leader forward. During this time, leaders are encouraged to reflect on themselves, their institution, and their leadership practices.

- The coach must take the role of "learner" to ensure that ownership of the process and the responsibility for leadership development rest in the leader's hands.

- Active listening is one of the most powerful, but also most under-used, skills of coaching.

- Effective questioning will prompt reflection on practice.

- Questioning needs to be at different levels to encourage reflection about educational beliefs, the goals for the institution, and the social and political context.

- Reflection that focuses on one's educational platform is an important part of leadership development.

- Knowledge of the educational context of leadership is paramount to an effective coaching relationship.

Coaching the skills
that move leaders forward

CHAPTER OVERVIEW

Once the coaching partners have established trust and understanding, the coaching process needs to move into more formal self-assessment procedures designed to promote goal setting and action planning, and allow ongoing observation of practice leading to descriptive and evaluative feedback. The skills involved in this process and their relationship to the change process, with its underpinning of action research, form the topic of this chapter. The descriptions of the skills are again accompanied by activities.

Self-assessment

Self-assessment is another extremely important aspect of an effective coaching relationship. The coaching partners must continually remember that responsibility for learning lies in the hands of the leader being coached. The coach must always invite the leader to first self-assess after any given observation visit or reflection on progress towards goals. Doing this helps the leader learn how to clearly identify his or her strengths and areas needing further development.

Many institutions have self-assessment frameworks in place, such as within performance appraisal, and utilise professional standards or capabilities as a basis for these. The headings used for these may well be suitable for self-assessment of leadership practice. However, self-assessment can also be linked to external assessments involving, for example, development centres and reviews.

Table 4 presents self-assessment topics set within five suggested frameworks, any of which can be used to guide self-assessment at the beginning of the coaching process.

Self-assessment guidelines and process

- The first self-assessment process should take place during the very beginning stages of the coaching relationship. Leaders need to set aside quiet reflection time to do this, individually and then with their coaches.
- Self-assessment needs to occur after each shadow observation and during all subsequent coaching sessions. At these times, the leader and the coach need to take time out apart from each other to reflect on the strengths displayed and the areas for further development or lost opportunities for achievement of goals. In this way, self-assessment becomes part of the whole evaluative feedback process.
- Self-assessment needs to focus on leadership practices that will work towards the achievement of professional goals.

Activities to build the skill
Reflective activity 10

The self-assessment that forms this activity is important as you begin to take ownership for the areas that you do well, for identifying when and how your leadership practice aligns with your professional goals, and for determining when you need to put more development work into certain areas.

A) Use any one of the five frameworks given in Table 4, or another that your institution may use for self-assessment or that you develop, and reflect quietly for 20 to 30 minutes on your work.

TABLE 4: FRAMEWORKS USEFUL FOR GUIDING SELF-ASSESSMENT

Framework One[a]	Framework Two[b]	Framework Three	Framework Four[c]	Framework Five

• Vision and leadership
• Building community relationships
• Striving for excellence
• Self-efficacy
	• Professional leadership
	• Strategic management
	• Staff management
	• Relationship management
	• Financial and asset management
	• Statutory and reporting requirements
		• Strengths in leadership
		• Areas for development in leadership
		• Specific focus on student achievement
		• Specific focus on team building
		• Culture-building aspects of leadership
		• Specific goal for research
		• Professional development goals
			• A conceptual job description
			• Leading, co-ordinating and facilitating the learning community
			• Managing and developing the culture
			• Taking responsibility for communications networks
			• Playing a figurehead in representing the institution
			• Personal professional development
				• SWOT analysis (personal and professional):
				  – Strengths
				  – Weaknesses
				  – Opportunities
				  – Threats

Notes: Adapted from:

[a] Hay Group (2001), *Identifying the skills, knowledge, attributes and competencies for first-time principals: Shaping the next generation of principals,* Melbourne, Hay Acquisitions Inc.

[b] Ministry of Education (1998), *Interim professional standards,* Wellington, Ministry of Education, Retrieved 1 February 2005 from: http://www.minedu.govt.nz/

[c] Stewart, D. (2000), *Tomorrow's principals today,* Palmerston North, Massey University Kanuka Grove Press.

B) When using the framework, focus specifically on the smaller individual goals set, or use it as an overarching assessment of your leadership practice in your institution.

Reflective activity 11

Here, you are required to set a specific focus for leadership development or the achievement of a goal. For example, you might want to look at how to make more effective use of colleagues' strengths in group meetings, or how to get colleagues to take responsibility for shared goals.

A) After the shadow observation session, conduct your self-assessment by taking careful reflective note of anything you did during the session that moved you towards your goal. Also note missed opportunities or areas where you felt you could have done better.
B) Elicit feedback from your coach after the session, as this will provide further valuable material for your self-assessment reflection.
C) Now review your goals.

Goal setting and action planning

After, or as part of, the self-assessment and related reflective interviewing session, goal setting, followed by action planning, can begin. Goal setting enables leaders to look ahead and determine desired outcomes. Goals can be personal or professional, individual, or institutional. The goal-setting process establishes a framework for the professional support necessary to achieve goals. It gets leaders to focus on the specific leadership actions necessary to achieve long-term outcomes. Leaders need to critically reflect on what it is that they want to achieve before they can work on related action plans. They also need to understand how their daily actions ultimately impact on their ability to realise desired outcomes.

Goal setting arises most naturally out of self-assessment sessions that are effective. "Effective" means that goals are reviewed and monitored and that dialogue centres on leadership practice. Leadership goals should usually be established in more than one area of the leader's work. Just what these areas are will depend on each leader's institutional context. Some examples are:

- teaching responsibilities;
- research;
- business development;
- community service;

- curriculum responsibilities;
- department or institution-wide responsibilities;
- entrepreneurial activities; and
- contract outputs.

Having identified the relevant areas, leaders should take each one in turn, setting goals for it with the support of the coach, before going on to the next one. The coaching partners also need to establish what indicators will help assess progress towards achievement of goals. Identifying time frames and situations or dates where the coach can give feedback are also important parts of the process.

During goal setting, the coach acts as an outside facilitator, as a conscience and a guide who keeps the focus and impetus firmly directed towards the achievement of goals. The coach helps the leader monitor progress towards the goals. Research reveals (see, for example, Robertson, 1995; Winters, 1996) that when leaders consciously align their leadership actions with their professional goals, they naturally enhance their own and others' self-efficacy, which in turn allows desired change in the institution to occur more rapidly.

"Probably giving us direction and making us more formalised; to actually get something done and achieved rather than just chatting. ... It's goal setting. I think you probably keep drawing us back to that."

Goal-setting guidelines and process

As stated in Chapter 6, the GROW model provides a particularly useful means of structuring a coaching session around goal setting. The model,

TABLE 5: HOW TO USE THE GROW MODEL WHEN GOAL SETTING

GOAL	REALITY	OPTIONS	WRAP-UP
• Agree topic for discussion • Agree on specific objective of session • Set long-term aim if appropriate	• Invite self-assessment • Offer specific examples of feedback • Avoid or check assumptions • Discard irrelevant history/information	• Cover range of options for future action • Invite suggestions • Offer suggestions carefully • Ensure choices are made for future actions	• Commit to action • Identify possible obstacles • Make steps specific • Define timing • Agree on support needed from coach, others, or professional development

Note: Developed from M. Landsberg (2003), *The tao of coaching*, London, Profile Books, p. 31.

to use Landsberg's (2003) version, involves four simple steps: Goal, Reality, Options, and Wrap-up. As a reminder, Table 5 sets out how to use each of these steps in a goal-setting session.

During goal setting, the coaching partners need to:

- Set achievable but challenging tasks.
- Keep the coaching focus on helping to formalise the structure of any goal-setting session and helping the leader work consistently towards achieving the goals.
- Allow sufficient time for leaders to reflect individually on what their professional goals are for the following year or years.
- Think "behind" each goal by asking: What factors will facilitate/restrain goal attainment? (For more on this, see Covey, 1990.)
- Build self-efficacy. Popper and Lipshitz (1992) claim that the coach can facilitate this process by performing four tasks during goal-setting:
  - Identify and define clear parameters of success.
  - Build and structure situations that have the potential for success.
  - Identify factors that lead to success.
  - Identify inner sources of success.
- Remember that goal setting is both an individual and a shared activity.

Another useful tool for goal setting alluded to earlier in this book is Eaton and Johnson's (2001, p. 31) SMART process. SMART requires that the goals set are:

- **S**pecific
- **M**easured
- **A**chievable
- **R**elevant
- **T**imed.

Table 6 reminds you how SMART works and provides examples of questions that you can ask as you set goals in accordance with each of the SMART elements.

Once leaders have explored these questions, they should have a clear understanding of the goal, and some of the factors that will restrain or facilitate achievement. They should also have explored and discussed options for leadership actions.

Goal setting should ultimately culminate in action planning and leadership action. The overall process that coaching partners should follow when setting goals and attendant action plans and then assessing progress against them follows.

1. With each goal, establish indicators against which you can measure achievement and/or progress. (What will the situation look like when you have achieved this goal?)
2. Set an initial action plan—this sets out the first key steps towards achievement of the goal.
3. Set time frames for actions and goal achievement.
4. Determine where and when the coach will fit in to provide feedback and assist with the processes in the action plan.
5. Share and discuss the goal-setting framework with the coach, using the SMART questions to identify and discuss resources and barriers.
6. Implement the first steps of the action plan.
7. Monitor achievement. Use observation and feedback to guide the process.
8. Review the action plan in the next coaching session.
9. Act.
10. Monitor …

TABLE 6: QUESTIONS TO ELICIT SMART GOALS

Elements of SMART	Useful Questions
SPECIFIC (Make sure everyone knows about the aim.)	• What will you be doing when you have achieved the goal? • What do you want to do next?
MEASURED (Define standards to work towards.)	• How will you measure achievement of the goal? • What will you feel when the goal is reached?
ACHIEVABLE (Ensure that the goal is realistic.)	• What might hinder you as you progress towards the goal? • What resources can you call upon?
RELEVANT (Make sure the goal is worthwhile.)	• What do/will you and others get out of this? • Have the other parties involved agreed to it?
TIMED (Agree on a time frame.)	• When will you achieve the goal? • What will be your first step?

Source: J. Eaton & R. Johnson (2001), *Coaching successfully*, London, Dorling Kindersley, p. 31.

Activities to build the skills
Reflective activity 12

A) Select one of the templates on the next page and identify three major goals you would like to achieve while working with your coach.

B) Make sure you set goals in different areas of your work.

C) Work individually through the thinking behind the goal setting (use the GROW and SMART frameworks).

D) At your next coaching session, share this process with your coach. The coach's role will be to listen, question, and help you build on the SMART and GROW frameworks to develop these goals further, if necessary, and also the appropriate leadership action plans.

Observing and describing leadership practice

The opportunity to observe others enacting a similar role is, of course, an important predecessor of critical reflection and so must be built firmly into the coaching process. Observations should be authentic sessions that take place in leaders' own workplaces. If this is not always possible, they can be construed through role plays or by demonstrating certain leadership practices via vignettes in clinical coaching sessions. An effective observation session should be as much of a learning experience (albeit vicarious) for the coach as for the person being coached. Coaches need to give descriptive accounts of what they observe, and should neither judge nor interpret the observed behaviours. However, leaders also need to acknowledge that observing and describing someone else's practice is inevitably somewhat subjective in nature and should guard against this subjectivity when describing their partner's leadership practice. Understanding and confronting this consideration are part of the process of developing the skills of observation and description.

Essentially, observing is not about judging whether the leadership practice in focus is good or bad, effective or ineffective. Nor is it about the coach telling their partner how they would act in a similar situation. Unfortunately, this is what coaches most often like to do! But it is not part of the coaching model set out in this book.

Observing and describing the guidelines and process

There is no one right way to observe practice. The coach and leader will develop what works best for them, in their context. The shadow

TEMPLATE ONE

Goal:

Results expected: By when?
-
-
-
-

What support can the coach give to assist you to achieve this goal?
-
-
-
-

TEMPLATE TWO

Goal setting within a conceptual job description (adapted from Stewart, 2000, p. 171)

Responsibility 1:
For example: Lead, co-ordinate and facilitate the learning community

Concept:
For example: Establish and maintain [institution] where learning is a highly valued activity by all members of the community.

Key Objectives	Results Expected	Professional Standard
....	....	....
....	....	....
....	....	....
....	....	....

What support can the coach give to assist you to achieve this goal?

....

....

....

....

observation may be as short as a one-hour meeting or involve three days in the institution.

When shadowing and observing a leader in action, the coach needs to:

- Gather information about the leader's practice.
- Provide a *descriptive* account of the leadership practice.
- Use this as a legitimate opportunity to see another leader in action.
- Remember that this is a privileged position and so must take an ethical stance that encompasses trust, loyalty and confidentiality.

The coaching partners need to decide together:

- How they will carry out the shadowing observation.
- What data will be gathered and who will see this material.
- How long the session will be.
- When the session will be.
- Where it will take place.
- What specific focus it will take.
- What feedback is necessary and from whom. (Feedback can come from other people and sources, for example, student evaluations, community consultation, and "360 degree" feedback.)
- What the ethical implications might be. (For example, should permission be sought from staff to observe a staff meeting and take notes? How can people's anonymity be guaranteed?)

During each observation session, the coach must note:

- Observable events (e.g., "Looked at watch five times"; "OHTs could not be read from back of the room").
- Key quotations and main points of conversations (e.g., "You said, 'I am totally mortified by this!'").
- Non-verbal communication (e.g., body language, placement of chair).
- The physical environment.
- Time intervals, if important (e.g., "Spent three minutes on phone").
- Names of people involved in interactions.
- Points that specifically relate to the goal and focus set.

After the session, the coach needs to:

- Take time to fill in the notes taken during the observation.
- Do this before meeting with the partner to give a descriptive account of what was observed and then follow through with the reflective interview.

Activities to build the skill

The following pen-and-ink activities will give you some guidance on types of teaching or leadership practices and behaviour to look out for when observing your partner and how to describe these to him or her. Facilitators can employ these activities in similar ways by using video-clips or role play in workshop sessions and then by asking participants to describe the practices/behaviour that they observe. These descriptions can then be shared one by one, with the group evaluating whether each practice involves a judgement/interpretation or a straightforward description. This is a very powerful way of assisting leaders to see how much people's own values, beliefs, and practices influence their view of the work of others in their institutions.

Reflective activity 13

A) Which of these statements contains a judgement/interpretation (J) and which is a description (D) of the observed behaviour? For each item, circle either J or D.

• Mary responded favourably to your suggestions.	J / D
• You divided the staff into four groups and set tasks for each group.	J / D
• You spoke for 10 minutes at the beginning of the meeting.	J / D
• I liked it when you asked each staff member to respond.	J / D
• You asked Peter to take notes from the discussion.	J / D
• It frustrated you when Peter took too long with the feedback section of the meeting.	J / D
• You asked each group leader to provide one piece of evidence.	J / D
• You were anxious to complete the meeting.	J / D
• You dominated the meeting.	J / D
• Your Powerpoint presentation was good.	J / D
• Each person in the group contributed to the discussion.	J / D
• You were poorly prepared for the meeting.	J / D
• Your Powerpoint presentation included goals, actions, and outcomes.	J / D

B) Discuss your answers with another leader, group of leaders or your coach. What sorts of ideas and thoughts do you now have about the observation and description of practice?

Reflective activity 14

This activity involves the coaching partners workplace shadowing. (If you think it is useful to do so, look back at "An example of a reflective interview", page 101 of Chapter 7, which gives examples of questions related to strategic planning.)

A) Set up a workplace shadowing session.
B) Decide on the specific leadership practice that will form the focus of the session. An example might be: "Building staff's commitment towards and ownership of the institution's strategic plan."
C) Conduct the session, with the coach observing closely and taking careful notes.
D) Set time aside after the session for the coach to give descriptive feedback and the leader being observed to identify the leadership practices that led towards the goal and those that did not assist in goal achievement.
E) Arrange a time for the leader to share these thoughts with the coach.
F) Now go to the giving evaluative feedback guidelines and process immediately below to see how the observation and description of practice are important components of the full evaluative feedback process.

Giving evaluative feedback

Giving evaluative feedback is quite different from descriptive feedback, but follows after it, and after self-assessment of the leadership practice. It involves the coach giving the leader professional advice and considered judgement and critique about his/her leadership in terms of making effective progress towards desired goals. It is important that the coaching partners negotiate guidelines for the process. These should be written down and a copy placed in the coaching folder (discussed in Chapter 6) for further reference. With any evaluative feedback session, sufficient time must be set aside for the feedback process to occur. It can be very frustrating for leaders if there is not sufficient time for their coach to give adequate feedback on the leadership practice observed.

Evaluative feedback guidelines and process

Effective feedback:

- describes leadership behaviours (that can be changed);
- is specific, descriptive, and informative;
- is related to the leadership goals and the focus set;
- makes links to the long-term goals and how this session fits into the overall aims of the coaching partnership;
- takes into account the needs of the leader and leaves the leader's dignity intact;
- is well timed and given as close as possible to the time of the observation;
- highlights successes and is positive about the ability to improve practice;
- is understood in the way it was meant; and
- gives specific examples of areas for improvement or further focus.

The first step in the feedback interaction is for the leader being coached to set a focus *before* the observation takes place. The partner being coached must be the one who directs what is to be observed so he or she can obtain the feedback required from the coach. The focus can be quite general ("Please watch me take a staff meeting or group meeting") or specific ("I'd like you to evaluate how effectively I use the expertise of the Board at the meeting next week so that they take on specific responsibilities"). The focus should also be consistent with achievement of the long-term goals set earlier.

"I should have had [coach] do a reflective interview on some point, but he had to get back to [institution], and I wouldn't have had any feedback if I hadn't asked for it. There is little point in having learnt the skills to put to some useful purpose if we don't use them."

The second step of the process is careful observation, and the recording and describing of behaviours as described previously. After the observation, the leader and the coach should each take a few minutes to reflect on the leader's actions during the session, and make brief written assessments of their thoughts. The coach's notes should include comments on positive and negative aspects of the leadership just observed, and should be couched in terms of progress towards goals. The leader should include in his or her summary assessment those actions and behaviours that helped achieve the set goal, and those that could have been done more effectively or developed.

After approximately five to 10 minutes apart, the leader and coach again meet together. The coach *describes* the leadership behaviours noted during the interaction, while the leader listens. For the leader, just listening to this description—the body language noted, the words used and the leadership actions—gives the leader a new awareness of his or her actions and so greatly enhances self-reflection.

When the coach has finished giving all of the descriptive feedback, the leader self-evaluates, presenting both the positive and the negative, while the coach actively listens without interrupting until all self-assessment has been completed. The coach then gives the leader *evaluative* feedback, pointing out the positive elements first and then the areas for development. The leader actively listens to the feedback in its entirety and does not interrupt, justify or explain. Finally, the two leaders discuss the session, explain and articulate reasons for comments and actions, make suggestions, bounce ideas around, set new goals together, and plan for the next session.

In summary, the evaluative feedback process involves this 10-step approach:

1. Leader establishes an area of focus.
2. Coach observes the leader in action (refer back to the skills of observing and describing).
3. Coach takes careful, descriptive notes.
4. Coach and leader take five to 10 minutes apart to prepare notes on the observation, setting these down according to:
   a) Strengths—what worked well; progress made towards goals.
   b) Development—what could have been done better; what were missed opportunities.
5. The pair again meet up.
6. Coach *describes* what he or she observed, and the leader actively listens (refer back to skill of actively listening), without interruption.
7. Leader self-evaluates (coach actively listens without interruption), giving his or her reflection on strengths and development.
8. Coach gives evaluative feedback (leader actively listening without interruption) on strengths and development.
9. The pair open up the session for reflective dialogue, involving questioning (refer back to skill of interviewing), discussion, and putting forward ideas.
10. Coach and leader review existing goals, set new ones (refer to the skill of goal setting), and plan out the actions needed to achieve them (action planning).

Note that *after* the leader has self-evaluated (Step 7), the coach may use a shorter version of giving feedback offered by Landsberg (2003, p. 22) and identified by the acronym AID:

Actions:	The coach describes the things that the leader is doing in the area under review.
Impact:	The coach describes the effect these actions are having.
Desired outcome:	The coach suggests how the leader could do things more effectively.

Of key importance is that the leader sets a specific focus in line with his or her professional goals, for the year ahead or for the specific interaction that week. Ensure sufficient time is set aside for the feedback process to occur. Also remember, as cautioned earlier, that leaders become frustrated if coaches do not utilise the skills they have learned of providing quality feedback and assistance with critical reflection for future action.

Understanding the change process arising out of action research

The skills described in this chapter and the previous one are essential for conducting action research as it aligns with the coaching process. Earlier chapters have outlined how the coaching process leads the leader into action research, with the coach as critical friend in the process. The point of this process is to help leaders reflect on their leadership practice and the context within which it operates in a way that allows them to determine and action changes in their practice and their institutions—for the better. Leaders need to be clear from the outset that this change process—the transformation of leadership practice and institutions—is the ultimate reason for the coaching partnership.

Action research involves the self-reflective cycle described by Kolb (1984) and discussed in Chapter 3 of this book. The cycles of development that characterise action research and underpin the coaching process are observation, reflection, planning, and action.

Action research guidelines and process

Leaders and their coaches need to remember that:

- action research is a change process;
- change takes place over time and is a *process*;

- leaders are *coached* into action research processes;
- action research will occur naturally if the coaching sessions are carried out regularly over a period of time;
- the change process needs to be made overt to educational leaders; and
- leaders must understand how the change process operates at the personal level and the institutional level.

The action research process as it relates to coaching is detailed in Chapter 5, so does not need to be reiterated here. However, a couple of further comments concerning the process can be made at this point. From the outset of the coaching relationship, coaching partners need to work together to ensure they are both fully aware of the change process underlying action research. When coaches encourage and help their partners to see how their many actions, small and large, work together over time to bring about achievement of long-term goals, they not only gain greater understanding of the change and development process but are also assured that progress is being made.

This understanding and assurance can be heightened when coaching partners join with other leaders engaged in coaching. Partners might find it possible to join up with another pair of coaching partners in a region, or perhaps a group of leaders in a cluster group who are also coaching partners, or even within a department that has established professional coaching. Group sessions are enriching because they allow leaders to hear about the coaching projects and goals of others, to reflect on their own coaching partnerships and skills, to exchange ideas and support, and to take part in group problem posing, problem solving, and action learning.

An activity to build the skill
Reflective activity 15

This activity helps leaders develop an understanding of the change process at the personal level, and also gives opportunity to review Kolb's (1984) learning cycle.

A) Individually: Think of a time when there was a huge impact on your life—either professionally or personally.

B) Jot down what happened. Was it a change of job or country? Was it the loss of a loved one? Was it a promotion that you were not ready for? Was it a personal grievance taken out against you?

C) Answer each of the following questions:
  - How did you feel at the time?
  - What did you then do?

- What did you do at a later point of time?
- How were you then different?

D) In pairs, or with your coaching partner, take turns at sharing your critical incident and related thinking. Use the skills of active listening.

E) Now share another incident with each other and reflect on and answer the questions listed. Use the skills of active listening and reflective interviewing to link your incidents with values and beliefs about your institution and your vision for it.

F) After your time with your partner, self-reflect, using these questions to guide you:
- What has this activity taught me about the change process?
- Can I relate this to Kolb's (1984) learning cycle of concrete experience, reflective observation, abstract conceptualisation (coming up with new ideas), and active experimentation (with new ways of being)?
- Can I relate this process to an example of institutional change?

SUMMARY OF MAIN POINTS

- Listening and reflective interviewing are two of the most important skills of coaching.
- Leaders must remain responsible for their own learning.
- The leader's context is unique to the leadership practices being coached.
- An ability to describe practice effectively and to give and receive feedback on practice is important in effecting long-term desired change in leadership practice and in the institution.
- Coaching leads effectively into action research processes, with the coach as critical friend.
- Groups of leaders engaged in coaching partnerships heighten the sharing of ideas and theories on education innovation, thus forming professional learning communities.
- Knowledge and understanding of the change process and how it is promoted by action research are essential for effective coaching.

Troubleshooting
and monitoring
the coaching relationship

CHAPTER OVERVIEW

While coaching is generally a beneficial process for all participants (see, for example, Robertson, 1995), problems can occur. Today's market-driven education system constantly works, in various ways, against leaders' ability to undertake the type of collegial professional development, such as coaching, that will allow them to develop the critical leadership so vital to the effective operation of their institutions. This chapter outlines key factors that inhibit the success of the coaching relationship: lack of time; the guilt leaders experience in devoting time to leadership development; their perception that coaching may denote a deficit in leadership practice (or that others will think so); the fallout from loss of coaches and confidence; and the importance and difficulty of changing established practices. As a counter-measure to these difficulties, this chapter also stresses that effective reflection on and action learning regarding the coaching process will help partners work through problems that do arise. The most important thing is that the relationship remains strong. The leader must feel that the coach is genuinely committed to their work and the leadership development.

Difficulties

Lack of time

In recent years, educational leaders have had to accommodate many new, time-consuming responsibilities into their everyday leadership practice. These responsibilities have come about as a result of government policy that educational institutions should be self-managing. Leaders involved in the leadership coaching research studies mention over and over again the lack of time to get everything done and feel that this lack is one of the main reasons preventing them from pursuing their own ongoing professional development. As one leader emphatically commented in an interview:

> [It's all about] TIME—to get together. TIME—to think reflectively. UNFORESEEABLE INTERRUPTIONS—the exigencies of the service throw up barriers to achieving all we want to in terms of getting together.

Another leader focused on the irony of time constraints, saying that the time when he most needed his coach's support was the time when he was under the most pressure and so was either unable to access that support or, if he could, to utilise it effectively or enjoy it.

Comments from other leaders involved in the leadership coaching research studies reveal that they often are in reactive rather than proactive mode, responding to the demands on them, to use Barth's (1986) analogy, like doctors in a busy accident and emergency clinic. I certainly encountered many such demands during my observations of leaders in the research studies. The following are just some of the ones that forestalled planned shadow (observation) visits:

- external deadlines;
- an angry parent arriving unannounced;
- meeting with social welfare officials;
- being caught up with the police on a suspected physical abuse case;
- taking the caretaker to the hospital because he was experiencing a heart attack;
- taking a class due to a teacher's absence and no relief staff available;
- a planned student protest; and
- a newspaper phoning to get a comment on future staffing losses.

In one institution, one issue was so dominant and so volatile that the leader was dealing with one crisis after another. This situation dominated any efforts to think about other matters in his institution, and he found it very difficult to concentrate on setting any professional goals or to see any value in shadowing his partner. He told me the issue was so "overriding" that he had not been able to do his normal work.

Guilt

Lack of time more frequently sees leaders thinking they are indispensable, which contributes to them feeling guilty about taking time out for their own professional development. They fear that they might be letting others in their institution down while they are away, or that something "bad" will occur. One of the leaders in my doctoral research study actually stated that his staff and community considered that he was away too often, and he lamented, "Something always seems to happen when I'm away." For some leaders, feeling guilty also related to their belief that, having attained a leadership position, they should not require further professional training and development. The extent to which leaders felt guilty depended on their individual personalities and circumstances. One rural principal, for example, acknowledged his feelings of guilt, but commented, "It's getting easier to leave school. I am learning to trust my staff and realise that the place won't fall down without me."

"This is my release day. Perhaps I should be at school working on my administration?"

The notion of deficit

The feeling of guilt aligned with the belief that leaders should not need further professional development ties in closely with the view of two leaders in one research study who considered that taking part in coaching indicated some sort of deficit or deficiency on behalf of the leaders participating in this process. One of these two told me that some of the people obviously got a good deal out of coaching because of what she termed "overt personal problems." She initially felt that the openness with which these leaders talked about the issues and dilemmas facing them in their institutions was a sign of deficit, but then she later realised that it was because this group was more open and honest about their leadership concerns than were other groups of which she was a part. She stated that many principals maintained a bluff and that behind the bluff were often ineffective leaders. She also reflected on the lack of hierarchy in the group and how everyone listened and learned from everyone else. She observed that often it was the younger, less experienced leaders who had the best ideas.

The other leader who held the deficit viewpoint was her coach, and he admitted that he had discussed the coaching with his board. He told me laughingly that they had thought it was a bit of a joke. "One of the board members," he said, "laughed and asked, 'Is [partner] developing you or are you developing [partner]?'" This type of attitude from a governing body is, of course, hardly conducive to setting the right culture for lifelong learning, and it is interesting that this leader also took the longest period of time of anyone in the group of leaders to begin to reflect on his own practice. However, he later said he valued the coaching sessions with his partner from a neighbouring school and commented, too, on the importance of maintaining that professional sharing and collegiality within a climate of competition between schools.

Loss of partner

Given that effective coaching relationships take time to develop, the loss of a coach can be a real setback for a leader. Stress-related leave and retirement are just two of the reasons why one person may leave the relationship. Faced with the imminent retirement of his coach, the leader concerned found it difficult to maintain allegiance to the partnership and to discuss his long-term goals with the coach. This inevitably undermined the pair's coaching relationship during their final sessions. In one of the stress-related instances, the prolonged absences of the partner made it difficult to establish a bonding relationship. A leader who took early retirement because of stress-related illness did not share his concerns with his coach, even though they had been working together for nearly one year. The day the leader made the decision that he could not face going on with his job was the same day he had been to his coach's institution to carry out a shadow visit.

Loss of confidence

To break established habits and confront their own leadership, leaders have to move out of the comfort zone of taking their everyday practices for granted, but this does have risks, and loss of confidence is one of them. "Navel-gazing", to use one leader's description of in-depth reflection on practice, initially can cause leaders to lose confidence in their ability to lead, especially when, as should be the case, they confront their own leadership style rather than simply working with their partner to problem solve day-to-day issues. Any loss in confidence needs to be carefully and sensitively worked through by the coaching partners. An outside facilitator working with the two coaching partners is generally a good addition to the professional development at this point.

Loss of confidence may have been one of the triggers that caused two principals to resign from principalship during one of my research studies. Their interview transcripts portrayed a growing disillusionment with education generally and their own inability to adjust to the changes being thrust upon them. One of the principals took early retirement and allowed me to interview him three months after he had left his school. This is what he told me:

> I just found it was taking me longer and longer to do everything, and I wasn't doing it as efficiently as I was three years ago ... I felt like I was dabbling in this and dabbling in that, and felt like I just needed to shut my office door and sit down and write ... the whole thing blew up in my face after a morning in [partner's institution]. It was a good morning. [But] I just got back and looked at the piles of paper and said, 'What the hell was I doing?'

When I asked him whether he felt there was any connection between the two events—visiting his partner's workplace and then coming back to his own and feeling that he could not continue—his answer concerned me, as it indicated a loss of confidence combined with a lack of fulfilment in his new role of self-management:

> Yes, I think that is very true. I'd had a good morning in [partner's institution]. He was interacting with students, and I went back and said, 'I'm not doing enough of that.' I got back and just saw two monstrous piles of paper, and then my board chairperson dropped in and wanted something straight away and I thought, 'This is the last straw.' That was it. It put me over the top.

This leader did say, however, that he felt coaching had helped him. He said there were times when he felt he could not afford the time but still made the commitment and was always pleased he had. "It was very worthwhile," he said, "to get away from that paper, so it depends where you put your priorities." Coaching had assisted him to see himself more clearly by observing his colleague. And while he did not like what he saw and became demoralised, coaching appears to have given him the impetus to think more clearly about his situation, both personal and professional, and to make the decision to leave. While this may not be an intended outcome of coaching, sometimes from personal, professional and/or institutional perspectives, it can be the right one.

Established habits

The coaching model requires leaders to work in ways that are very different to the way they usually interact with one another, and it requires them to use skills that they are not in the habit of using with their professional colleagues. New ways of operating can be a problem for leaders, and they can easily slip back into old habits of just conversing with their coach and not carrying out the processes of reflective interviewing and giving evaluative feedback. This is where the deliberate presence of a facilitator can help "institutionalise" some of these new practices between leaders. (For more on this facilitation process, see Chapter 10.)

"I feel that we are at the stage now that you have set us up, and we are carrying on, on our own."

Outside factors

The many other events going on in leaders' lives will affect the amount of time they are able to commit to coaching. These factors are those that occur over and above the day-to-day happenings of leaders' institutions. They include family commitments, secondment to other positions, community conflicts, external reviews, and external deadlines. Coaching comes into its own here because effective coaches can assist leaders to prioritise time and work more effectively around the unanticipated or extra events that will inevitably occur in their personal and professional lives. Dealing with interruptions and the unexpected is the very essence of the work of leadership, and helping a leader see that this is so is one of the main benefits of coaching.

Lack of attendance

While group sessions can provide near ideal conditions for the development of coaching skills, coaching partnerships, and learning communities, illness or pressure of work can make it difficult to convene and develop a community of learners. The programme needs to continue, but with special compensatory visits paid to the absent leaders. They, too, will feel their absence has placed them at a disadvantage. Said one leader: "At the moment I feel very lost. Why? It's a pity I did not attend the first meeting. Result—I feel like I am now catching up—trying to catch up."

Counter-measures: The art of critically reflecting on the coaching relationship

For all the leaders in the research studies, the successes of coaching far outweighed the problems. However, these leaders were also cognisant of the difficulties inherent in developing, and then maintaining, an effective coaching partnership for the purposes of their own professional development. To sustain a coaching relationship long term, the partners need continually to monitor and evaluate their work together. In other words, leaders improve their leadership *in* coaching, *by* coaching. The following activities aim to provide leaders and their coaches with ideas on how to talk about and reflect together on the coaching process itself. The coaching partners may also find it useful to have an outside facilitator involved in a critique of this kind. And they are likely to find that their learning will be greater if they can move into the double-loop learning (Argyris, 1982, 1999) that occurs as a result of encouraging outside perspectives.

Activities to build the skill
Reflective activity 16

This activity requires you to look at the depth of your professional dialogue by reflecting on your answers to these questions:

- What topics do you talk about?
- What is difficult to talk about?
- What is easy to talk about?
- What don't you talk about?
- How honest can you be?

Reflective activity 17

Now take a look at your coaching styles, and then reflect on your answers to these questions:

- How would you describe the coaching style?
- What works best for you?
- What is least helpful?
- What is the most important coaching role?
- What new learning has there been?
- How have you changed?

Reflective activity 18

In regard to the coaching relationship:

- How do you feel the coaching is going?
- Is it professionally fulfilling?
- What problems have you experienced?
- In what ways could you improve the relationship?
- Any other comments?

Reflect on your answers to these questions.

Reflective activity 19

Now think about and reflect on your answers to these questions:

- Do you carry out a "formal" reflective interview each time?
- Why? Why not?
- What causes the most reflection on practice?
- What is the most beneficial part of time spent together?
- How useful is the reflective interview?
- How would you describe your experience of the reflective interview?

Reflective activity 20

It is important that those of you in coaching roles keep a reflective journal to support your own development as a leadership coach. The guidelines in the first point below are adapted from those that Zeus and Skiffington (2002, p. 87) outline for their "coach's notebook". The ideas in the second point on the next page are those which leaders who have been utilising the "Leaders Coaching Leaders" model in their work and graduate study for a Master of Educational Leadership qualification have found useful.

1. Record the following in relation to each goal set and write reflection notes in relation to these items.

   Goal: What does the leader want to achieve?

   Time-frame: When does s/he want to achieve it by?

   Steps: What steps should be taken? How can I assist?

   Results: What happened? What progress is being made?

   Issues: What new learning has there been for me?

   Reflection: Where to from here? What links can I make to anything I have read? What else could I do to assist? What sort of feedback can I get from the leader about the coaching process?

2. Include in your journal:
   - Ideas from readings (e.g., "The relationship takes time to develop", Robertson, 1997).
   - Exploration of concepts (e.g., praxis, reciprocity).
   - Chronology of contacts/correspondence with leader/s.
   - Reflections on your role as coach/facilitator.
   - Reflections on your new learning.
   - Quotes or communication with leader/s (e.g., an email or comment made that seems significant).
   - Evaluation of the coaching sessions.
   - Skills development (e.g., ability to get closure in sessions; use of GROW model).
   - Session ideas for working with your partner.
   - Anything else you think is relevant.

SUMMARY OF MAIN POINTS

- Many factors, whether personal and professional, and internal or external to the institution, can adversely affect the development of an effective coaching relationship.
- Awareness of these factors is the first step in countering them effectively.
- Monitoring and reflecting on the coaching process is the second important step in countering difficulties and strengthening the coaching relationship.
- Coaching *is* a relationship—and focusing on the process of developing that relationship must be given prominence throughout the coaching process.

Facilitating coaching

CHAPTER OVERVIEW

Facilitating and coaching are almost synonymous in this coaching model, given that the coaching style the model promotes is facilitative rather than instructive. Coaching partners facilitate each other's leadership development, while a third person engaged from outside the partnership specifically to take on the work of a facilitator coaches the coaching process. The coach and the outside facilitator take a somewhat different focus when acting as facilitators, but to be effective both must be able to facilitate learning and to assume various roles to varying degrees. This chapter describes and discusses these roles primarily from the perspective of the outside facilitator.

Facilitative roles within the context of coaching

Although peer coaching will develop effectively between two colleagues who are committed to a reciprocal coaching process, or will develop between an external coach (e.g., a retired principal, an adviser, a consultant) and an educational leader, coaching is a process that benefits from outside facilitation. This is particularly the case when the coaching is between groups of leaders, such as in one department or one cluster, or involves establishing a coaching relationship between a business partner and educational leader, or between two different groups in networks. Because facilitating coaching is about coaching the coaching process, rather than coaching leadership development, facilitators need to have experienced the process of coaching, to understand learning and leadership theory, and to be conversant with the change process. Facilitators can come from within an institution or from outside.

"You [the facilitator] have had to work to get to the level the group is at now. People trust you and reveal, in the small group, small personal items related to their leadership. We trust each other."

People who facilitate the coaching process have the challenge of lifting the learning relationship between coaching partners to higher levels of critical thought and dialogue than are perhaps possible without this outside perspective. In the course of their work, these facilitators become involved not only in the coaching process per se but also in coaching partners' individual, partnered, and group professional development processes. They also, inevitably, take on many and varied roles, some of which leaders have colourfully termed "flea", "taskmaster", "the glue", and "devil's advocate". While the names given to the facilitator roles that follow are far more prosaic, they capture the essence of the facilitator's work and are the roles that Everard and Morris (1985) deemed important in their work on consultancy. These roles are "process facilitator", "dynamist/motivator", "exemplar/demonstrator", "pace-maker", "reminder", "learning facilitator", "coach/tutor", "consultant", "resource investigator", "co-ordinator/convenor", "catalyst/assumption challenger", "group dynamics advisor", "norm establisher", "observer/note-taker/scribe", and "discussion leader/task facilitator". Two additional roles, namely "advocate" and "confidant", arising out of my own research and development work with leaders, are also pertinent here.

The different roles

Process facilitator

One of the facilitator's most important and obvious roles is that of facilitating the whole process of coaching, including the initial bringing together of the coaching partners. Because of the nature of their work, leaders are very unlikely to move into coaching relationships unless someone else encourages them to do so. As one leader said, "In a way, setting up ... is a very difficult thing to control because of the demands of the job."

Once the coaching relationship has been established, support is necessary to sustain it. Facilitators accordingly keep leaders moving towards attainment of their professional goals and help them become increasingly autonomous in the coaching process. Most leaders relatively quickly display an ability to set directions and goals and work together towards these on their own, but may still welcome the outside facilitator's "guidance—keeping us on track" and "following through" from time to time after he or she has facilitated the early sessions. Encouraging the coaching partners to stay with the process can be as simple as the facilitator asking such questions as: "Tell me again, what is your goal?" "What are you going to do next?" "How will your coach assist in this process?"

Dynamist/motivator

The facilitator's own enthusiasm for coaching can be a source of dynamism—of revitalisation and refreshment—especially for educational leaders in mid-career. Dynamism stimulates, and stimulation motivates leaders to maintain their coaching relationships and work through the coaching process. Motivation of this kind can also come from other leaders involved in the same coaching processes, whether they are part of cluster groups, learning communities, or institutional departments.

For leaders, stimulation often stems from the fact that somebody else is taking a keen interest in their practice. In other words, interest acts as a motivator. The interest that coaching partners show in each other and their leadership

> *"I've thought of you as the glue in the whole business of giving direction, encouragement, knowledge and structure to the types of contacts that we have had between each other ... . The most effective thing is you—that glue—because without it I don't really think it could exist. I don't think it would be as effective if you removed yourself from the situation."*

practice also acts in this way, but interest is given added impact as a motivator when it comes from an outside facilitator. While the person who ultimately takes the ongoing interest in a leader's leadership practice is that leader's coach, the interest of the outside facilitator provides the necessary impetus for leaders to carry through their goal setting and action plans. This impetus might take the form of providing the partners with ideas and with an affirmation for things going well, of challenging them to think about their leadership and the process of coaching ("What is the most fulfilling part of your coaching so far?"), and of sharing one's own experiences of being coached.

Exemplar/demonstrator

The principles of coaching serve to bind all participants in the learning community to the same processes. With facilitating, this consideration translates into "Do as I do", not just "Do as I say." Here, facilitators must model the role of a coach and, as part of this activity, must discuss the benefits and issues they face or have faced when working through coaching processes with their own coaching partners. They might choose, for example, to share practical ideas of what works in their own coaching process, or to share how they worked through an issue of concern. Facilitators who describe and discuss with others how they and their partner coach each other offer valuable practical examples of how coaching operates. Educational leaders who have established and are carrying out the coaching process for their own professional development have validity. Their expressed and modelled belief that coaching promotes educational leaders' professional development is seen to be sincere.

Pacemaker

Facilitators take on the role of pacemaker when they help keep leaders to a time frame for prioritising actions, set the next steps of action plans, check that skills have been practised, and tasks have been carried out, set dates for future coaching sessions and meetings, and suggest a next step or something else the coaching partners could try before the next full session. One of the leaders with whom I worked as a facilitator told me that she saw my pacemaking role as not only providing a support but also acting as a conscience and a guide throughout the coaching process. She said:

You are obviously the facilitator. We definitely look to you for support. To some extent you are a compelling force because I know that you are going to be there, and therefore I feel, "I must do that 'cause I'll be seeing Jan," and I don't want to go and say that I haven't done it.

When helping set the pace of the coaching, facilitators also need to nudge leaders along by, as one leader put it, "making polite suggestions" as to what they ought to be doing, "with the hope that we will take up the suggestions." She also signalled another aspect of the pace-maker role when she commented to her facilitator: "You bend over backwards to get us to do something, to change."

Reminder

At times, coaching partners slip back into previous modes of operating. For example, they may resort to discussing rather than challenging, using few, if any, of the coaching skills they have been taught, and neglecting to reflect critically. This is where facilitators serve as reminders, by helping coaching partners refocus on the skills they need to use or ways they can work together to enhance the likelihood of achieving their professional goals. Here, a facilitator might ask the partners if they have carried out the reflective interview they planned to do, or remind them of the guiding principles of giving evaluative feedback.

> *"It is easy to just relax and forget what we should be doing next, instead of keeping just a little bit more formal. Not formal, but just thinking things through a little bit more."*

Often, coaching partners' familiarity with each other will work against their ability to move into the more formalised modes of interaction that coaching requires, as this leader's comments show:

We are together the whole time. You think about the time that you stopped and talked to me and then you left me by myself, and I could stop and think about it and plan my next action, as opposed to us just talking and me responding to the moment, not stopping and thinking about it. I think that is why it was not happening for me, and because we talk together like that all the time, you forget the obvious things.

Reminding leaders about "the obvious things" is the essence of the reminder role, as is drawing their attention to whatever they had agreed to attend to before or during their next meeting.

Learning facilitator

One of the facilitator's most important influences on the developing coaching process is that of teaching leaders about leadership development and clarifying for them how the process contributes to it. For most leaders, working with a professional colleague in the type of coaching relationship employed in this book's model will be a new experience, and so the facilitator needs to introduce them to the skills they need to carry out the process effectively. For those leaders who move more easily into the mode of working with a partner to set and implement professional goals and then monitor and evaluate their progress, the facilitator's teaching role will increasingly become one of highlighting new and different opportunities for enhanced leadership learning to take place. At times, however, facilitators can find it difficult to know when (and when not) to intervene in this way, but skilled facilitators can usually judge when to introduce a "learning moment" and when to leave the partners to learn from their concrete experiences. Knowing the right questions to ask, and when, is also a valuable tool in the facilitator's "learning" kit.

Here is an example of how one facilitator provided coaching partners with learning opportunities. In this instance, the partners had met for a reflective interview, but instead of employing the appropriate skills, they got sidetracked into general conversation. At this point, the facilitator intervened, again rehearsed with them the skills of reflective interview and encouraged them to proceed accordingly. Afterwards, the facilitator held a discussion about the intervention with the leaders, checking with them why they had not utilised the reflective interviewing technique, and asking how they felt about the intervention at this point.

> *"In skilling us in terms of how to conduct a reflective interview, those types of things—the imparting of those abilities and skills—I think it has been really, really terrific."*

Coach/tutor

The role of learning facilitator inevitably encompasses another role, that of coaching and tutoring the skills that leaders need to coach each other successfully. Facilitators take the role of coach whenever they observe leaders and assist them to practise taught skills. Examples here are demonstrating how to conduct a reflective interview on a particular issue and asking leaders who have completed a reflective interview to identify the Level 3 questions (see Chapter 7) that they asked their partner.

When teaching leaders skills and then coaching them as they practise those skills, facilitators may choose to work with those leaders individually, in pairs or in groups. Leaders often need individual tuition on aspects of coaching that have not quite gelled with them or when they have missed a coaching session. At such times, the facilitator as coach is akin to a personal trainer—someone who is able to identify and target a leader's specific professional development needs.

Consultant

Educational leaders seldom have the benefit of people, knowledgeable in both the theory and practice of education, who have time to sit and talk with them about larger issues in education and educational institutions. When facilitators engage with leaders in this way, they are acting in a consultative role. They bring to discussions a knowledge of theory that complements leaders' practical leadership knowledge. The close association that forms between facilitators and the coaching partners with whom they work allows facilitators to gain a clear and detailed picture of the leader's professional needs and the way in which that person works towards goals. This understanding, in turn, allows facilitators to tailor their consultation to the leader's needs and chosen areas of focus. This assistance might involve professional dialogue about the day-to-day issues of leadership and dealing with staff, introducing some new perspectives about the next steps in the leader's action plan, sharing a knowledge of research literature relevant to an issue at hand, or providing advice on how to run professional development workshops for staff. Essentially, the role of consultant is one of helping leaders to help themselves, and it can be employed at an individual, group, and institutional level.

"I asked them to look specifically to outcomes for each of their schools for that year. One leader's reaction was to laugh (he didn't have any!). The other said, 'I had one in the back of my mind.' It made me realise the importance of leaders sitting and doing this exercise and then asking them, 'Do your staff know these outcomes?'"

Resource investigator

Because facilitators generally have a broad-sweep knowledge of education and educational issues, and because their work sees them range widely across the educational community, they have a good knowledge of particular resources that leaders may find useful as they work towards the achievement of their goals. Resources can range from research articles and websites on a particular educational matter to other leaders within a coaching community who have grappled with and found solutions to certain problems. Sometimes, within the context of a coaching community, a facilitator may suggest that a leader with knowledge or experience of an issue acts as a consultant to another leader or coaching partnership.

Providing knowledge from professional sources is a way of linking theory to practice and practice to theory. The role of resource investigator offers an effective way to affirm and/or challenge leaders' practices. During my research, one leader with whom I was working as a facilitator said another leader had asked him to evaluate the culture of his (the other leader's) institution. In discussing a framework he could use for the evaluation, I was reminded of an article called *Good Seeds Grow in Strong Cultures* (Saphier & King, 1986), and I promised to send him a copy of some material in it. "It's got some really good norms for culture building in it," I told him. "I think it's relevant for you, because, look at the seeds here, he has asked you to do the evaluation because of your strength in this area."

Co-ordinator/convenor

Leaders do not have sufficient time to establish and organise professional development sessions for themselves (Robertson, 1991a). The work of setting dates for future meetings, circulating meeting agendas to leaders to add to and reflect upon, and organising speakers and consultants in relation to specific professional development matters is essential in establishing and maintaining coaching partnerships and fits readily within the facilitator's scope. Facilitators' knowledge of appropriate resources and appreciation of the limited time that leaders have available for professional development means they are well suited to setting up sessions that will bring maximum benefit to the participants. However, facilitators should not be complacent about what they provide. At the end of each session that they convene, they should ask participants to comment on what they found valuable/not valuable.

Catalyst/assumption challenger

In creating the conditions that are conducive to change, facilitators will assume the role of catalyst. The observations and the reflective interviews of coaching are the most obvious opportunities to instigate change in leaders' practices. Facilitators can also use group sessions to create the necessary conditions for change. The actual agenda of a group session can be organised around whatever the facilitator thinks is necessary to advance the coaching process and/or the leadership skills of the group. Facilitators may take on the role of consultant during these sessions, or bring in someone else in this role. Sessions will not work unless the activities used within them (e.g., role plays) are appropriate to the needs of the participants and the identified focus for the session (e.g., skill practice, developing a community, setting professional goals, developing action plans). Nor will they work if the participants fail to work together as a "team" to identify and articulate their values, and to utilise the strength of these values in pursuing their professional goals and bringing about changes in their leadership practice.

"I think there is somebody that has to have an overview, coming in with other ideas, because you see many more leaders than the partners do, because they only see one, but you see the lot."

The most successful sessions are those that challenge leaders to confront their leadership practice and the beliefs and values underpinning it (their educational platform). Facilitators can act as challengers because they bring in the perspective of an outsider. The leader-as-colleague/coach is often too close to a particular situation or issue to provide the objectivity required to challenge certain ways-of-knowing. One activity that brings in challenge is that of role playing a contentious issue and then critiquing what went on and was said during the role play. Another is conducting a session relating to various aspects of the political and social context of education and then having leaders critically evaluate the impact of those aspects on their leadership.

Group dynamics advisor

During group sessions, the dynamics of the group need to be conducive to the developing coaching relationships. Leaders are most likely to work well together when the session takes place in a venue that is warm, quiet, and comfortable, and away from the distractions of their daily practice. There should be no phone calls or other interruptions. Music can be a part of these sessions, and food should always be provided. The one thing that the leaders who participated in my earlier research studies (see, for example, Robertson, 1991a) mentioned more than any other was enjoying the opportunity at tea breaks and lunch to talk to their colleagues. Leadership coaching is about capturing that energy and dialogue, and building on these.

Another aspect of developing group dynamics is the affirmation that educational leaders are important people and that their commitment to the coaching model is valued. These points need to be made explicitly, but never patronisingly, to the group. Group dynamics are further enhanced when facilitators remind participants of how group dynamics operate. As such, the first in a series of sessions or the early part of a one-off session should contain activities that will help participants understand how they can use the dynamics of the group to collectively advance their aims. If time is limited, simply emphasise the importance of everyone having an opportunity and responsibility to participate, and highlight that groups are less effective when they try to achieve consensus about, rather than a true understanding of, an issue.

Norms establisher

"I enjoyed or benefited from [consultant's] session because he gave us a strategy that we are reluctant to use in a 'conflict' situation. Perhaps we need to be told that some strategies are OK."

The way the group operates, the success of a coaching partnership and the relationship of facilitators with leaders will all be more effective when norms or expectations for behaviour and conduct are established early on. The most important ones are trust and confidentiality. For example, leaders will share much more of a personal nature with their facilitator on an individual basis if they know that the facilitator will never reveal what is said to the full group or others with whom they work. Norms of openness, honesty, and support should also be established.

These norms are basically those that come under the heading of "Professional Ethics", and should be discussed and committed to before the group gets underway with the work at hand. The group also may choose to draw up principles to work to as a group, such as being open to ideas and willing to learn. Another important norm is that of the purpose of coaching— professional leadership development. All sessions should focus on this, and the facilitator may at first need to keep explicitly reminding leaders of this norm because it is one that is rarely evident in the other groups within which leaders meet.

> *"You never reveal anything about us back to the group. You don't just assume that would be OK."*

Observer/note-taker/scribe

Observing and note-taking are primary tasks for the facilitator. This work may involve noting down things that the leaders have decided to do, or perhaps observing how the leaders are working in their coaching relationships. It may also, importantly, involve writing down, in the form of short case studies or case records of goals and/or issues, how leaders develop the theory of their own leadership within their work.

Another consideration here is that leaders are often reticent about, or too busy moving onto, their next action to write anything down. The notes that a facilitator makes are only useful if they are sent as soon as possible after the observation to the leaders for their feedback and comment. Leaders find this outside perspective particularly useful in helping them reflect more critically about the processes in which they are involved. It lets them see their actions from another angle, and it gives them an opportunity to think about what they do in relation to theory, and then to see how their practice influences and becomes theory.

> *"I'm most impressed with all this. You write it down, and I read it back, and it sounds different, but that is exactly what happened.*
>
> *The key word is 'emancipated'. 'Counter-hegemonic'—I like that! I am never sure how to say that word, but that is exactly what it was!"*

Discussion leader/task facilitator

At group sessions, in particular, facilitators often take the role of discussion leader and task facilitator by setting topics for discussion and then "chairing" that discussion. Facilitators often choose topics by listening to leaders talking about what is important to them. Performance contracts and related objectives, and personnel generally, are always timely topics. Another is the dilemmas leaders face over review and monitoring in their institutions. In regard to the second topic, leaders could work through the task of analysing the issues related to reviews, looking for leadership actions and strategies that would best suit their individual circumstances. But whatever the topic, it is important to ensure the discussion has a critical perspective and takes account of the current educational context. Good facilitators will chair the discussion in a way that allows everyone present to bring their knowledge to the situation and to hear the different views within the group.

Confidant

It is interesting that Everard and Morris (1985) did not identify the role of confidant, given that it can be one of the most important facilitation roles. This role is integral to facilitating the change process. Change begins at the personal level, and unless the facilitator comes to know the coaching partners as individual people, then it is unlikely that the intimacy and reciprocity required for openness, development, and a more in-depth account of what is actually happening in the coaching partnership will occur. Leaders generally also require the active listening of a confidant to move into dialogue and problem posing. Facilitators who, during the first 10 minutes or so of the coaching session, actively listen as the leaders talk about the issues and dilemmas they are currently facing are likely to establish a very useful rapport very quickly.

"Coaching also engendered some self-doubt for me, and the facilitator's role as a confidant and conduit in providing relevant readings (e.g., Southworth, Clunie, & Somerville, 1994) helped allay some of those doubts."

Advocate

A graduate student recently pointed out to me that another important role for the facilitator, and the coach, too, for that matter, is that of advocate. The inside knowledge that facilitators and coaches have of the practice of individual leaders places them in a prime position to speak up for these leaders at interviews, performance appraisals, and conflict situations. A coach, in particular, can also act as mentor and sponsor in highlighting career opportunities for their partner, and assisting them to meet career goals. Good coaches advocate for their partners where possible, perhaps by bringing a job advertisement ("This as written for you!"), or speaking out in support of them in a professional situation.

- The facilitation of coaching involves many important roles.
- The coach can play each of these facilitation roles for the educational leader.
- Outside facilitation is often necessary to initiate the process of coaching between two people.
- Outside facilitation can also enhance the professional coaching relationship.
- Groups of coaching partnerships can be developed together with the aid of a good facilitator.
- Effective facilitation requires critical reflection on the continuing process of facilitation and coaching.

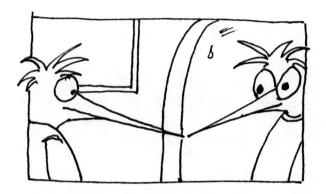

Leaders coaching leaders

CHAPTER OVERVIEW

Once leaders have experienced coaching themselves, they move easily into developing coaching practices with their colleagues. For these leaders, coaching has moved to a new level, that of *facilitator*— of coaching others to use coaching skills. This development promotes the building of effective leadership capacity throughout an institution. The case studies presented in this chapter tell the stories of three recently qualified coaches, each of whom worked in different ways with their professional colleagues to facilitate the skills of coaching. Each story is told in the leader's own words and is followed by a brief commentary.

Three case studies

The first case study (Case Study 1) presents the story of an assistant principal who worked with two experienced women leaders in her school. She was genuinely surprised at how little she knew of these women and their work. She was also pleasantly surprised at how committed they were to the development of their leadership and how much they valued her own expertise and interest in them. Case Study 2 focuses on a principal who worked with two principals in his local principals' association group, while Case Study 3, conducted in a tertiary institution, tells of a head of department who invited three colleagues in similar positions to practise and use coaching in their leadership development.

Taken together, the studies highlight that experience of coaching gives leaders confidence to work with others to develop their skills of coaching and their own skills of facilitation. More importantly, facilitating coaching allows leaders to reflect on the change process and enhances their ability to use an action research process to guide their coaching. (Facilitation of coaching was dealt with fully in the previous chapter.) The leaders tell their own stories here.

CASE STUDY 1: Assistant principal facilitating coaching in her own institution

I facilitated the development of educational leadership with two of my work colleagues based on a peer coaching model by Robertson (1997). I was working as an assistant principal in a large intermediate school, with approximately 1,200 students. The two colleagues I chose to work with were mature women, experienced teachers, in some ways lacking in self-confidence yet seeking to extend their leadership capacity.

The aim of the facilitation of a coaching partnership was to give the two participants the skills, attitudes, and behaviours to become more reflective about their practice and, in doing so, to develop their leadership skills and add to the focus on quality of what was happening in our school. I also wanted to help provide these two women with a sense of personal importance, significance, and work meaningfulness, and motivation as described by Sergiovanni (2001).

The basis for trust and respect between us was established through having worked together for the previous seven years. However, the basis for trust was not taken for granted and was furthered from the outset by agreeing on the ground rules. A statement of ethics was signed by us all, and the women were assured that it was my facilitation of the process which was important, not what they had to say. We practised to develop skills in context such as observation, reflective interviewing, three-level questioning and active listening. Once trust was established, the two women observed each other's practice, with a set focus, followed by reflective interviewing.

The facilitation of leadership skills through a peer coaching model occurred intensively over a two-month time span. Meetings between the three of us were held weekly, before or after a work day, mainly on the work site, but sometimes over breakfast downtown. The dates for meetings were set in place from one meeting to the next to ensure that they happened amidst our busy daily lives. Meetings were formalised and purposeful, as I was appreciative of the amount of personal time these women were prepared to sacrifice. Meetings were a vehicle for any issues the participants wished to raise and involved readings to encourage fresh perspectives.

As a facilitator of the development of leadership skills in others, it was necessary to take on various roles, similar to those suggested by Robertson (1997), and to have the ability to move in and out of them. These roles included relationship builder, motivator, planner, pace setter, encourager, advocate, goal setter, task facilitator, scribe, conscience, observer, confidant, and conversation starter. It was important that I was sincere, enthusiastic, and motivational.

When reflecting on the facilitation of the leadership skills process, it was important that I come from the position of coach and not mentor in order not to destroy the confidence of the participants but to further empower them. I did not want them to feel I was telling them what to do or how to do it. Taking the time to reflect on practice through formalised arrangements was absolutely powerful. Both participants exclaimed they never otherwise took the time for reflection. I was somewhat surprised by this reaction, as I had taken for granted that structures were already in place to provide the opportunity for reflection. This highlighted for me the importance of a facilitator for reflective practice to occur.

The participants agreed that they felt empowered in their leadership practice through their improved ability to question. Acting in a non-judgemental way was crucial to the success and continuation of this coaching partnership. Both felt it was affirming to have the positives. One of the women commented that she had been "waiting for the punch" because that was what she was conditioned for. Knowing when and how to feed in the evaluative feedback was crucial to the success or otherwise of our partnership. For me, this coaching model has the potential to empower teachers by giving them input into their professional development and can assist participants in career development as suggested by Ehrich (1996).

> *Commentary*: In highlighting the additional roles she played, that is, conscience and conversation starter, this leader extended coaching theory. As the two women's senior manager, she was well aware that power relations could impact negatively on the coaching. She therefore stressed the importance of sincerity in the coaching process, and worked hard to encourage the women to take responsibility for their own learning, and ownership of the power arising out of that learning. Her role as facilitator of critical reflection was particularly important in this respect.

CASE STUDY 2: Principal facilitating coaching partnerships in a professional community

A supportive and trusting partnership was established with two principals in local, urban, low-decile schools. The intention of this professional partnership was to recognise and appreciate the uniqueness of each principal's circumstances and then, through an agreed, structured process of reflective questioning, to utilise our collective capacity to assist each person to reflect and deal with the various types of challenges pertaining to their daily management and leadership roles.

The process was undertaken during 10 sessions set aside specifically for this exercise. The standard agenda had those involved sharing their leadership stories and then developing skilful questioning to analyse each other's issues without being judgemental. Skills of active listening and reflective interviewing were fostered to enhance maximum learning opportunities for these principals. Developing these skills helped support our coaching by providing a framework for interactions, reflection, and shared understanding.

The initial meetings were one on one, allowing the facilitator to explain the intention of the coaching, time, and task commitments, along with the probable long-term benefits from their involvement. Opportunities were also given to allow any personal resistance, or concerns related to possible anxiety or insecurity, to surface. Meetings first took place in each other's schools, then at the agreed neutral environment of a city café. Meetings lasted on average 90 minutes and followed an agreed format:

– Coffee and general downloading of what had been happening at school.
– Identifying significant issues to be shared.
– Reviewing of partner's questioning and coaching role to be practised during discussion.
– Undertaking the sharing and questioning process.
– Identifying possible options for action to support the resolution of an individual's issue.
– Discussing possible indicators that may suggest the issue is being resolved.

Having this agreed approach to facilitating supportive discussion fostered a greater appreciation of each individual's leadership context while enhancing trusting relationships within our professional partnership. The professional development was also supported by the facilitator supplying a range of research articles on professional coaching. The facilitation of this professional leadership partnership challenged the way those involved thought of, and undertook, their leadership roles. The process also refocused participants on the behaviours and the positive attitudes required for effective leadership.

The learning undertaken through the process has better prepared those involved to "walk the talk" as reflective practitioners. The strength gained as a result of this positive collegial and collaborative experience has fostered a support network that addresses the increasing concern of professional isolation felt by principals.

Those involved recognise the value of supportive dialogue to encourage risk taking and promote the importance of connecting theory and practice. Through regularly discussing quality education and effective leadership, there now is an increasing openness to new ideas. Simply, our increased professional bond has formed a social context of group learning.

Developing professional partners should be considered an effective way to support professional development, while decreasing a feeling of professional isolation. It challenges school leaders to transfer behaviours of active listening and reflective interviewing into the context of their daily roles, thereby developing behaviours designed to enhance the collective ability of a school to adapt, solve problems, and improve performance.

As principals, we need to consistently engage our staff, community, and students in the decision-making process. To achieve this we need to facilitate our own learning opportunities and those of others within the context of our schools. We need to be fostering partnerships to bring the vision of our schools to life, by utilising the collective capacity of others as we continually seek to improve the quality of our schools. "Walking the talk" through "professional partnerships" is one successful way of developing and practising the skills required to achieve this.

> *Commentary*: This leader's experiences demonstrate how coaching can become a three-way relationship when one principal coaches two others in the skills of coaching for their leadership development. He constantly mentions the importance of collective ability and the collective capacity that accrues through working together to solve shared problems. He sees coaching as the route to achieving a true learning community. This principal also emphasises the importance of "walking the talk"—of leaders needing to start with their own development, and the development of others in their institutions. Recognising the professional isolation that educational leaders experience, he emphasises the importance of working with colleagues in similar positions to construct knowledge through collegial dialogue focused on issues of mutual concern.

CASE STUDY 3: Head of department undertaking peer-assisted leadership with three colleagues in a tertiary institution

I became interested in the concept of peer mentoring in a variety of educational contexts. As I read more on the topic, I considered the possible benefits to my colleagues and me in our leadership roles in a New Zealand tertiary institution. I discussed the idea with several colleagues and established a small group of three [other heads of department] as a pilot study—all of us women, and all with varying degrees of leadership experience. The study was partly to complete an assignment but also to help my own professional practice as an educational manager.

The process was to develop a series of partnership discussions that related to the immediate educational leadership needs of my colleagues. I decided that I would follow a similar pattern to that used by Robertson (2004a) in a "Leaders Coaching Leaders" process. This entailed me acting as coach and establishing ground rules for the discussions, providing literature about peer mentoring, and organising the sessions. We agreed to meet once a week for six weeks and evaluate the sessions at the completion.

The first session began with an introduction to the concept of peer-assisted leadership, and we discussed some of the issues which related to the leadership role, particularly reflective practice and the role of a critical friend (Costa & Kallick, 1993). The partners engaged in the active listening process and continued to do this for the next five sessions, practising and refining their ability to listen to their partner without interrupting and breaking into their own stories, to reflect on their daily tasks and to discuss dilemmas and professional practice. At the conclusion of the first session, we made a series of times for the next six weeks, and agreed to remain flexible but to stick to the schedule wherever possible.

The next five sessions were structured to allow a time at the outset for reflection on the previous week's reading or information that I had shared with the partners. There was generally an "instruction-style" time also at the beginning of each session where I outlined the purpose of the session and checked with the partners that they were happy with the process. The partners then discussed issues about their work, which included performance management, staff issues, curriculum developments, or topics which had created dilemmas, joys, or difficulties for them. Each session concluded with me giving a summary of the discussion and asking for feedback on the process.

Issues for our partnership included: making the sessions meaningful, time management, the role of the facilitator, and value for participants.

Meaningful sessions

I had to resolve how to make the experience meaningful for the partners. Which activities and skills should we practise, in which order, and what would be relevant? The information gained from the classes where I was being coached in a partnership with another class member was essential to guide my decision making and planning for the sessions. I also had to decide which readings and articles to give my partners, and to assess whether they would see the reading as an extra chore, an imposition on their precious time, or a valuable part of the peer-mentoring process. My colleagues would often pick up on something I was explaining and ask for some more reading matter on that area. For example, during the discussion of experiential learning theory, I was asked if I could give some readings to help the HOD in her discussions about practical fieldwork for a particular group of students. Another issue discussed related to dilemmas in appraisal, so I was able to provide reading material regarding that issue.

As I read more about educational leadership, I became more concerned and aware that there is little focus in our work environment on the "real" leadership issues. In this business-focused environment, HODs are encouraged to be "budget-oriented" and to have a sound knowledge of resource management issues. There is little mention, however, of being a transformational leader, or about modelling the learning process, or creating cultures for learning. In these circumstances, I felt it was very important to provide my colleagues with interesting and relevant material that could be inspiring and motivational for them in their leadership.

Time management

Making time for the series of discussions required was a concern to me. All of us were very busy people, with one of the HODs responsible for 50 staff members and the other from a department undergoing major changes. Our work environment was fraught with difficulties and changes, and each of the partners had to make decisions about important human resources and staffing issues. Concern about the busy and complex nature of the roles of educational leaders is constantly raised in the literature, with the time factor consistently an issue for professional partners (Robertson, 1995). These partners were willing to put aside an hour each week, which was then often followed by lunch together. The leadership discussions often continued on into the lunchtime sharing sessions, and were noted as a valuable time for the partners and myself to build relationships and understanding of our lives.

Role of the facilitator

The role of the facilitator required careful definition and was important in providing structure and skills for the partnership. This included considering how to keep partners on track. Would they understand why I kept them focused on particular discussion topics? Through the facilitation role, I developed an understanding of the complex nature of being a mentor, or coach, at this professional level. I could identify the following roles that I played during the discussions: process facilitator, dynamiser/motivator, resource investigator, reminder (referred to also as "flea"), observer, note-taker, and confidant (Robertson, 1995). I also played the role of partner on several occasions when one of the partners was late arriving, and we practised active listening and reflective questioning as we discussed leadership issues. This was a very short six-week exercise, and we did not make the time to observe each other in the workplace context. I understand the benefits of further sessions for partners to actually shadow and observe their partner in their own work environment, which we have consequently undertaken. Seeing the other partner actually leading a team meeting, or undertaking an appraisal, was most useful.

Value for participants

It is important to create a climate of trust and honesty within the partnership process (Brady, 1996). I knew that this honesty and openness existed within the faculty team of HODs. At times, factors relating to personal development can hinder professional development, and individuals will react differently to change and improvement at different stages in their lives. Both of the HODs who agreed to be part of this pilot study were in an acting capacity in their role and had a similar number of months of experience in their job. One had completed her Master's degree, and the other had almost completed hers, so both were empathetic about the partnership project as part of my own university study. They were both keen to improve their practice in their leadership role.

The outcomes that are referred to in discussions based on peer-assisted leadership include the need for a greater focus on educational leadership based on reflective practice. The partners in my project both highlighted the fact that they had found this reflection very useful, and through reflection found they were becoming more aware of their own leadership style. The challenge for those of us who are leaders in an academic learning organisation is to provide effective leadership in a constantly changing academic and business environment.

The collegiality and support of their partner, whom they could trust with their stories from day-to-day experiences, were invaluable. One of the partners commented that leadership is lonely and fraught. Dussault and Barnett (1996) refer to this as professional isolation. For my colleagues, this partnership felt like a really safe place to practise skills and to know they were being listened to.

Commentary: This head of department, recognising that too little time is spent, particularly in tertiary institutions, focusing on educational leadership, became a resource facilitator, carefully feeding into the process of coaching, and presenting research literature on leadership that would inspire and motivate her colleagues. Wanting the coaching process to be "meaningful", she constantly sought feedback on her facilitation of coaching. For this leader, the concrete experiences of being coached, and then reflecting on this process in the light of coaching others, were particularly valuable.

SUMMARY OF MAIN POINTS

- Leaders who have experienced coaching will more easily use this skill and knowledge to facilitate the process in others.
- Coaching other coaches builds leadership capacity within an institution.
- Coaching creates structured opportunities for collegial dialogue around shared issues.
- Leaders who facilitate coaching relationships between colleagues take on many roles.

Developing agency

CHAPTER OVERVIEW

Coaching relationships serve to strengthen the self-efficacy and agency of educational leaders. This chapter highlights how these two qualities in educational leadership align to instil in leaders the belief that they have the power to make a positive difference. This ability often entails working at the political level within an institution or national context, and is illustrated through a case study of a principal who used an Education Review Office review of his school as an avenue to bring about change. This chapter is also concerned with the premise that leaders will not act with agency on an ongoing basis unless they are equipped with the skills, support, and learning principles that allow them to constantly think about and re-evaluate the values and beliefs underpinning their respective educational platforms.

From apolitical to political

Critics of coaching would argue that the process simply perpetuates a situation whereby ineffective and apolitical leaders choose to work together and consequently fail to challenge their current ways of working. But my argument is that leaders will become politicised about the contexts within which they exercise the practice, to the point where they can act with agency, *if* the coaching model used disrupts leaders' usual modes of thinking and operating. The disruption must be one that discredits whatever "impressions" they have established of their leadership practice and the contexts within which it operates. The coaching model in this book provides this disruption in two ways. First, it requires leaders to work in different ways with their professional colleagues. Second, it uses the pressure exerted by the facilitator and/or the presence of the coach during workplace shadowing. The challenges and disruptions that facilitators and coaches bring to leaders' practice require leaders to question every aspect of what they think and do, rather than leaving it as everyday, taken-for-granted behaviour (Grundy, 1993).

The essential power of coaching is the ability of the coach to stand outside the situation and to ask questions about leaders' practice that challenge assumptions. When assumptions are challenged, leaders are able to revisit (critically reflect on) their educational values and beliefs and deconstruct their multiple roles. In so doing, they come to see that they are not alone, that other leaders face the same tensions and dilemmas. These insights lead them into looking beyond themselves to the bigger picture of their educational context. They begin to look at that social and political context with a more critical eye, seeing how their leadership roles are shaped by it. Realising that they no longer have to hide behind a façade, they begin to speak out about the tensions and issues they face, particularly to the groups of people with whom they work. This leads to shared ownership of the problems, to group problem solving, goal setting, and action planning, all of which are the ingredients of agency and empowerment.

One of the most important aspects of leadership develop-ment, then, is raising the awareness of leaders about the social

> *"I am probably less reclusive about what we are doing. ... I have become a bit more steely about those things [I believe in]. Having seen other institutions has fortified me in the way I'm doing things."*

and political contexts within which they conduct their leadership practice. As discussed earlier in this book, education is a political act, and educational leaders need to be aware of how public policy and directions impact on decision making within their institutions, so that they have the knowledge they need to act with agency. Neo-liberalism and its associated rhetoric of managerialism have placed educational institutions in the invidious situation of having to compete against one another as private businesses in a public service industry (Thrupp & Willmott, 2003; Wylie, 1994). Educational leaders need ongoing opportunities to debate the meaning of education, the effects of managerialism on educational institutions, and what it means to be part of the power structures that maintain the status quo.

As I discussed earlier in this book, my experiences with educational leaders on the coaching model have highlighted that leaders tend to employ a bluff exterior and "impression management" (Goffman, 1959) when working with their colleagues in professional situations. Given that educational institutions stand or fall on numbers of enrolments, it is not surprising that many leaders strive to keep up an impression of "everything is going well around here." This demeanour isolates leaders in their work and creates personal stress. Unable to share leadership issues and tensions with their colleagues, they believe that problems are entirely theirs, rather than ones commonly experienced by their counterparts. My research has also indicated that educational leaders often feel very exposed and vulnerable under the ever-watchful eye of colleagues and community—the "gaze"—to use Foucault's (1977) expression. They accordingly build up their boundaries with even more impression management and do not let anybody into the inner recesses of their institutions and practice. This façade, as I observed previously, is not conducive to institutional or professional growth, because issues remain hidden rather than being dealt with effectively.

Sometimes leaders situated within the challenging environment that coaching creates initially experience a loss of confidence in their existing practices, a situation that is also common in action research methodology. However, this loss of confidence acts as a catalyst for change because it, too, creates a disruption by nudging leaders out of their comfort zones and challenging them to look at their beliefs and practices from a critical perspective. The coach as critical friend and trusted colleague provides support during this time, encouraging leaders to set their reflection and goal setting in positive directions. Eventually, as goals are reached and new practices are tried, tested, and found valuable, leaders regain their confidence. Their lived experience of coaching shows them that this process and its attendant skills equip them to work more comfortably within the constant state of flux that is education today. It also shows them that they can act with agency; that they can bring about innovation in their own leadership practice and in the workings of their institution. Finally, it gives them the confidence to take risks. Acting with agency inevitably involves trialling new ideas and practices, some of which will succeed and some of which will not. What is important here is that leaders use both successes and failures as learning opportunities along the way to innovation.

The notion that coaching is an act of dissonance that leads to self-efficacy and agency is supported by the work of other researchers and commentators. Berger and Luckmann (1966) were among the first to propose that knowledge is socially constructed. They argued that change relies on creating dissonance within these constructions, and that dissonance is brought about by picking apart—deconstructing—through critical reflection and analysis. This picking apart creates new awareness or conscientisation (Freire, 1985) of issues and ways of operating, which gives rise to feelings of empowerment (the "knowledge is power" adage). Giddens (1993) refers to these feelings as agency—the notion that it is possible to act differently to how one has acted before.

> "Yes, definitely more assertive. [I now know that] my time is valuable. Therefore, when people waste my time, I do something about it. I know that if I can ... ask my [coach], 'Do you think I am right or wrong?' and that she would do things in exactly the same way, I can then say, 'I cannot agree with what you have done.'"

Bandura (2002) sees agency in terms of self-efficacy—the belief that one can make a difference. Gibbs (2002) highlights the importance of enhancing this belief in educators' professional development. Bandura, in his discussion of self-efficacy, highlights three types of agency—personal, proxy, and collective. Personal is agency conducted by individuals; proxy is where an individual enlists someone else to take charge and to make changes on his or her behalf; and collective is where a group acts together to achieve what they may not be able to achieve individually. The coaching studies highlighted that the coaching model favours all three types of agency. The studies also showed that the more self-efficacious leaders become, the more likely they are to commit themselves to directing their leadership practice towards implementing innovations designed to enhance learning and teaching within their institutions.

The following case study shows how one leader's experience of coaching gave him the self-efficacy to act with agency. Concerned about national policy matters that he believed would seriously damage the learning culture of not only his school but also other educational institutions in New Zealand, he decided to take a public stand on the matter. (This leader was the principal of a large, urban, intermediate school, and I was privy, as a facilitator-researcher, to his experiences at this time.)

CASE STUDY: One principal's stand

On receiving notification that the Education Review Office (ERO) would soon be conducting a review of his school, the principal decided to use this event as a coaching opportunity with his coaching partner. Having established the goal of "leading the staff positively through the review procedure", he asked his coach to assist him by "evaluating my performance in a non-routine type of school day—in terms of interacting with staff; the review team; the events of the day."

His coach had previously been through an ERO review, and he discussed proceedings with him and read the report that his coach had received from the Review Office. He also read through his own school's previous review report. He then talked with his staff and developed a plan of action.

The shadowing of the principal on the review day was planned as a professional development exercise for evaluative feedback on leadership performance. The principal later described the day as, "in actual fact … quite good because his school has recently had a similar review and they were able to involve him quite informally in the interview situation. … [Coach] basically sat there and just took his shadowing notes normally, apart from the fact that he was involved in it."

The review day was followed by a period of reconnaissance and critical reflection. This began with the coach carrying out a reflective interview, a description of leadership and a verbal feedback session after the reviewers had departed for the day. He later gave the principal concise descriptive notes on his observations of the afternoon with the reviewers. The principal, while then reflecting on the actions of the review day and about education generally in New Zealand, remembered something he had heard at a conference some years earlier: "The focus has changed again, just a little bit more, and it is getting back to what Ivan Snook [refer Snook, 1990] warned us about at our 1989 Intermediate Schools Conference. He said that you are going to be required to provide education like sausage manufacturers fill sausages, and it will be inputs and outputs and no allowance made for individuals. It is not quite like that, but it is very strongly, 'How do you define achievement for the whole school and in particular in these areas?'"

These thoughts led him to think further about his educational philosophy and the school's achievement statements, and to gather new insights. Then, reiterating that he felt good about the review day because he had "clearly known the school, the staff and the programmes that go on within it," he began reflecting more deeply about the realities of his educational leadership. On the one hand, he said, was the reality of his educational leadership requiring him to work with senior staff who were not as effective as some of the assistant teachers in the school. On the other hand was the reality of his having to take two hours out of the review week to try to get painters to remedy an ineffective job they had done in the school, an effort on his part that he cynically saw as "in some obscure way contributing to the advancement of the educational cause."

The report of the effectiveness review duly arrived from the Review Office, and the principal told me, while I was conducting an interview for the research study, how he felt when he received it. He said that he particularly "took objection to the phraseology, 'the board of trustees is unable to demonstrate …'." He then discussed this issue with his coach and told him that he, personally, was not going to accept the review in its present form, and that he hoped he was going to get the support of his Board for this decision. His discussions with his Board led to the support he wanted: the report would not be accepted as was. When I asked him whether he thought this action would be the best one for the learning of the children in his school, he replied that this very consideration was how he measured the worth of his actions. He then said that during a discussion with a group of intermediate school principals on the way to an association meeting the previous week, concerns about ERO had surfaced. "We were saying, 'We've all been worrying about this Education Review Office outfit, and they are almost irrelevant. We are going to run our schools, and they can say what they like about it. As long as we are on the right track, as long as our values are correct, if they want to come in and criticise us, well, it doesn't matter."

These critical reflections spurred the leader on to take his next action. He contacted the manager of the local regional branch of ERO, stated he was not willing to accept the report and asked to meet again with the review team. This meeting was positive, and the reviewers agreed to alter the wording in the way the principal wanted.

The principal then began another period of reconnaissance (commensurate with the action research cycle described in Chapter 5). This included talking to other principals who had received reports around the same time he had received his. He found a particular opportunity to talk with his colleagues at a principals' conference. He not only talked with as many principals as possible, but also raised the issue of the phraseology of the report with two members of ERO who were attending the conference, as well as two ex-reviewers. One of the principals at the conference asked him for a copy of his report, as she also had a similar concern about the one she had received from a recent effectiveness review. It so happened that the chief executive officer of ERO was at the conference, and, overhearing some of the conversations, she spoke directly to the principal. He, confident in his convictions and the support of other principals, told her of the concerns that he had about the reviewing and reporting process, and she agreed to look into the matter. He later told me that the issue he raised about the negative and incorrect phraseology used in ERO reports "was discussed quite widely, and I got tremendous professional support, and as a result of that I think we have made a breakthrough on certain phraseology around the country."

When I asked him why he thought the issue he had identified was such an important one, he replied that he felt that wording in a report needed to be an accurate statement of fact—that it was not the fault of the Board of trustees that certain things could not be shown. Some of the areas were being newly implemented, as was a new system of assessment, and the fact that Board members were mostly laypeople who had nothing to do with the process, but were simply legally obliged to see that implementation took place, made the reviewers' criticism particularly unfair. The principal was also concerned that the press might get hold of this negative statement, and display it under a headline such as "SCHOOL UNABLE TO PROVE PROGRESS". Publicity of this sort, he said, could only "be bad for the school, bad for staff morale and bad for parent—school relationships."

When the amended report arrived, the principal said he was pleased with the changes made. He reflected that ERO did have a role to play in ensuring accountability in schools in New Zealand and now could see the report's relevance for his school's development plan. "Our system of recording data needs not only to show the added value but that we can use that recorded data to improve the quality of instruction and to add more value ... the action plan for this next year is to continue to fine-tune our assessment and evaluation."

Commentary

This case study demonstrates how the coaching process assisted one leader to confront the politics within his own education context and to gain a sense of self-efficacy—the belief he could do something about it. His anger about particular wording in the ERO report made him feel disillusioned about the whole Education Review Office audit, and he also felt disempowered as a result. He was concerned that the school might be seen in a bad light, by his colleagues and community, because of the wording in the report, and he was discouraged by the power of the media to potentially sensationalise the matter in the community. However, speaking to his coaching partner helped him look at the situation in a different light. Having been at the review days with him, she assured him his concerns were valid and that he had a strong point to make. He then took emancipatory actions (seeking support from his board and other principals, and challenging ERO officers) that released him, personally, from the practices he believed were not conducive to effective educative leadership.

At a more specific level, in reflecting on his initial reaction to the ERO report, the principal confirmed his understanding of the concept and practice of self-managing schools. Deciding that some aspects of the report were not true to that concept, he set goals and began a plan of action to remedy the situation. Having gained the support of his board, he consulted with other principals and eventually with ERO officers. This course of action meant that the effects of his actions went wider than his own school, to regional level, and then, as he said, "on to a national basis in terms of getting the phrases right—because it had to be cleared through head office." He agreed that it was "probably my lobbying" that resulted in ERO changing certain wordings in reviews. He added that he was not a political activist—"I have never been one of those"—but that he had felt so strongly about the issue that he had decided to act. In short, this principal became politicised: his actions had an effect on national policy and practice.

Through critical reflection of his actions, the principal became aware that he could act in a different way (agency), share the tensions and issues presented by the political context with his professional colleagues, and work to develop a united front to influence policy and practice. The whole process of developing agency allowed him to bring about the change he wanted. It also allowed him to view the players within the broader education context in a more measured, evaluative way, and to realise that a few words in the report had clouded his judgement about the worth of the Review Office. His admission that ERO did have a role to play in terms of accountability, and that the report's overall content would benefit the school, demonstrates his professionalism and political astuteness in his educational leadership role.

SUMMARY OF MAIN POINTS

- Leadership is an isolated role, and professional support through coaching can lead to greater feelings of confidence, self-efficacy, and agency.
- Educational leadership is influenced by social and political contexts, and leaders need opportunities to think about, and gain awareness of, their leadership roles within those contexts.
- Enhanced awareness promotes leadership as a political act, and leaders have a responsibility to take action on issues that are important.
- Coaching can lend the professional support and challenge necessary for critical reflection on leadership practice.

A FINAL NOTE

Beyond coaching?
Breaking the boundaries

As has been demonstrated in this book, coaching challenges and supports educational leaders to develop their leadership practice in ways that advantage them, their institutions and education. If all educational leaders had ready access to "coaching organisations" with "learning facilitators", how might the work of education be different? But given that today's leaders will be coaching tomorrow's leaders, there is the risk of getting more of the same in educational leadership and therefore educational institutions. What will always be needed to ensure leaders are constantly challenged into new ways of thinking, being, and acting are leadership programmes that work alongside coaching. Over the past decade, I have been involved in research with one such programme (see Robertson & Webber, 2002, 2004; Webber & Robertson, 1998, 2004). Based on what I and my colleague term the "boundary-breaking model", this programme provides boundary-breaking leadership development experiences that provide the support and impetus called for above.

Boundary-breaking principles

The incorporation of boundary-breaking principles into the way coaches and leaders work together provides the challenge necessary to move leaders from inaction to action, from reactive to proactive, and from perpetuating the status quo to challenging it. Coaching is thus a transformative process because it allows educational leaders to act with agency—to know they can contribute to and develop the system rather than be a cog within it. Surely this is the type of leadership that is required to meet the type of education demanded by the challenges of the 21st century?

The model is described fully elsewhere (Robertson & Webber, 2000), but what is relevant to note here is that it rests on eight principles deemed necessary to promote effective learning about leadership. These are:

1. *Developing a sense of community*: Requires promoting the personal wellbeing of leaders, ensuring that leaders have access to pastoral care, and that educational leaders are generous with their leadership in the sense that their focus moves from individual gain to advancement of the group. Such leaders create space for other leaders to take up leadership and give of their own time to assist them to do so.

2. *Including international perspectives*: Involves studying other education systems, policies, and practices on the premise that comparative studies aid critical reflection on issues (see Webber & Robertson, 2004).

3. *Using generative approaches*: Rather than engaging with a prescribed curriculum, leaders experience guided professional study of issues encountered in theory and practice.

4. *Validating personal knowledge*: Focuses on the notion that each leader brings valuable leadership theory and practice to the community from which all can learn as they construct new knowledge.

5. *Encouraging formal and informal leadership*: Considers that every leader has a responsibility and a right to take leadership within the learning group or the leadership team.

6. *Providing a forum for discussion*: Offers critique, debate and active participation as essential ingredients in the leadership learning process.

7. *Shared construction of meaning*: Maintains that developing understanding of concepts is a social process.

8. *Encouraging the growth of a counter-culture*: Puts forward possibilities and alternatives that are "deliberately at variance with the social norm" (*Collins Concise Dictionary*, 1999), thereby challenging leaders to consider, justify and articulate alternative ways of being and knowing.

Relationships between principles and effective coaching practices

These principles should also form the basis of effective coaching practices. Together, coach and leader can explore additional opportunities that place the leader in situations where the principles underpin the pedagogy. International study tours, visits to learning institutes, online discussion forums, conferences, and formal study programmes are all examples of learning endeavours that support coaching practices. Coaching provides leaders with the impetus, the conscience and the guide to try out new ideas gained in these forums.

When coaching partners employ the eight principles within their coaching process, they will find the following learning practices are a natural consequence (Robertson & Webber, 2000):

- *Co-learning*: Leaders can learn more (and achieve more) with others than they can from learning alone.
- *Public learning and teaching*: Leadership as learning in the public arena provides powerful learning experiences.
- *Flexible timing*: Learning can take place at any time.
- *Integration of technology*: Technology provides the space for and access to learning at any time and anywhere. The use of technology, so important to the boundary-breaking leadership model, can be harnessed for email communication, Internet resources, and video-conferencing. Together, these assist the face-to-face coaching process by providing an asynchronous and alternative mode of communication that offers leaders flexibility in their busy working lives.
- *Confluence of theory and practice*: Theory should inform practice as much as practice should inform theory.
- *Reduced control*: Leadership develops in contexts where it is encouraged to emerge and where leaders have to reduce their control or "give away" some opportunities of exercising their leadership so that others will take up responsibilities.

- *Shared/modelled leadership*: Validation of personal knowledge and generative learning approaches encourages the sharing of leadership, which should be modelled by those initiating learning opportunities.
- *Pastoral care*: The personal wellbeing of leaders is fostered through leaders' engaging together on learning on a professional basis.
- *"Possibilising"*: Possibilising is about creating "What if…?" moments in order to explore alternatives and ideas and where "ultimate hopes for the future are translated into action plans that seek to push out the boundaries of what is possible" (Halpin, 2003, p. 60).
- *"Big picture" focus*: This focus is gained when leaders have an opportunity to lift their heads up long enough "to climb the tallest tree to see what jungle they are in", to use an analogy from Covey (1989). It allows them to see the educational system as a whole and the part they can and do play in it, and it also allows them to distinguish between leaders and managers.

It is hopefully apparent from this book that the outcomes of the boundary-breaking model have direct relationships with the desired outcomes of leadership coaching.

Boundary–Breaking Model	Coaching
An emotional engagement with learning.	Deep learning moves leaders out of their comfort zones and established habits and ideas.
Movement beyond the self.	Vicarious learning and outside perspectives move leaders to a study of leadership practice rather than an examination of the self.
Development of a critical perspective.	Other ways of knowing assist the analytical assessment of leadership practices.
The development of agency.	Self-efficacy and confidence move educational leaders towards other ways of being—to acknowledging they are agents of change who can make things happen.

A powerful learning methodology

Essentially, coaching is boundary breaking because it is a powerful learning methodology. It allows for the development of a particular kind of organisational culture in which authentic learning and leadership are the two key components for all participants. West-Burnham (2004) believes, "The most powerful means of developing leadership is to create an organisational culture, which values the sorts of learning most likely to enhance the capacity of individuals to lead." He refers to the concepts of deep and profound learning. This is learning that is applied, and learning "where knowledge is converted into wisdom and where understanding becomes intuition." He believes that these two types of learning require two strategies to really make an impact: the opportunity to reflect, and coaching, which he states is "the essential learning relationship." He purports, as I have done throughout this book, that those who experience the coaching relationship with their colleagues bring these qualities and practices to their leadership and their work.

Duignan (2004a) similarly implores us to focus on leadership capabilities and heralds the advent of what he calls the "Capable Leader". In line with Duigan, I believe these leaders will be leaders capable of:

- constructing new leadership knowledge;
- creating boundary-breaking opportunities to gain critical perspectives and critical thinking; and
- crossing borders to new ways of being and knowing.

These leaders will also be caring, committed, concerned, and compassionate. They will be people who will have the courage to create opportunities for critical conversations (Robertson & Allan, 1999) centred on continual learning and improvement. They will be actively engaged in coaching—to build leadership capacity in themselves and in their institutions.

Support, along with challenges to current practice, are important elements to release this potentiality of the self and others. As Duignan (2004b, p. 2) reminds us, effective leaders

> Influence self, others and each other to: attain worthwhile and agreed goals; engage in meaningful relationship to generate and live a shared vision; use scarce resources responsibly; and elevate the human spirit through actions and interactions that are ethical, moral and compassionate.

Professional colleagues are well placed to provide these elements. Such communities of practice are built on notions of "colleagues as resource people." More often than not, the answers a group is seeking should and will be found by that group.

My research and development projects confirm that coached leaders value the chance to learn from each other and the leadership relationships they have within their institution as they create shared understanding and knowledge, and as they learn and model their leadership through their everyday actions. Educational leaders accordingly need to go on asking themselves:

- "How effective are we?"
- "How do we know?"
- "Where do we want to be?"
- "Do we need to change?"
- "How will we know when we have got there?"

Too often the word coaching is used ubiquitously and as a catch-cry, losing all relevance and meaning, because participants have no understanding of what it means to "coach". Using the skills described in this book, leaders can develop new ways of thinking and leading, and from there gain wisdom about appropriate leadership practice, or what Duignan (2002, p. 17) calls "gravitas"—knowledge gained from deep reflection on practice. This deep reflection can lead to insights that change the way even experienced leaders work in their institutions, as the following comment from Garry de Thierry, Principal of Rotorua Intermediate School, New Zealand, corroborates:

> Your leadership [coaching] programme has firstly had me reflect on my current beliefs and practice, then challenges me through research and debate to develop further as a leader … The whole process has got me away from an emphasis on management and towards a far better appreciation of the potential growth influence I can generate from being the school's educational leader. Thank you.

Garry's use of "potential growth influence" to describe the particular benefit he gained from being coached in educational leadership aptly highlights the transformative and innovative power for leadership practice of the coaching model. The development of the self, and operating at one's full *potential*, should always be the leader's primary focus. Professional development is about *growth* of the individual and the institution. Growth requires change and transformation, support and challenge. *Influence* is what leadership is all about—using one's position and energy to harness a collective capacity that allows for a shared vision. Everyone in an institution has the potential to contribute to that influence, and to influence that energy. As such, one of the most important roles a leader can take on is to recognise and engage the potential others have to contribute to the leadership energy in an institution—to take that institution on a journey from its current reality to a future that is desired and shared by everyone associated with it. Ultimately, coaching is the pathway to building leadership capacity of the kind that assists others to embark on that same pathway. I hope you enjoy journeying along it.

References

Alcorn, N. (1986). Action research: A tool for school development. *Delta, 37,* 33–44.

Apple, M. (1986). *Teachers and texts: A political economy of class and gender relations in education.* New York: Routledge & Kegan Paul.

Apple, M.W. & Beane, J.A. (1995). *Democratic schools.* Alexandria, VA: Association for Supervision and Curriculum Development.

Argyris, C. (1982). *Reasoning, learning and action.* San Francisco, CA: Jossey-Bass.

Argyris, C. (1999). *Knowledge for action.* San Francisco, CA: Jossey-Bass.

Bandura, A. (2002). Social cognitive theory in cultural context. *Applied Psychology: An International Review, 51*(2), 269–290.

Barber, M. (2002). *From good to great: Large-scale reform in England.* Paper presented at Futures of Education Conference, Zurich, University of Zurich, 23 April.

Barnett, B.G. (1990). Peer-assisted leadership: Expanding principals' knowledge through reflective practice. *Journal of Educational Administration, 28*(3), 67–76.

Barnett, B.G., & O'Mahony, G. (2002). One for the to-do list: Slow down and think. *Journal of Staff Development, 23*(3), 54–58.

Barnett, B.G., O'Mahony, G.R. & Matthews, R.J. (2004). *Reflective practice: The cornerstone for school improvement.* Moorabbin, Australia: Hawker Brownlow Education.

Barth, R. (1986). Principal centered professional development. *Theory into Practice, 25*(3), 156–160.

Bell, B., & Gilbert, J. (1996). *Teacher development: A model from science education.* London: Falmer.

Berger, P.L., & Luckmann, T. (1966). *The social construction of reality.* London: Penguin.

Berlak, A., & Berlak, H. (1987). Teachers working with teachers to transform schools. In J. Smyth (Ed.), *Educating teachers: Changing the nature of pedagogical knowledge* (pp. 169–178). Lewes: Falmer Press.

Bossert, S.T., Dwyer, D.C., Rowan, B., & Lee, G.V. (1982). The instructional management role of the principal. *Educational Administration Quarterly, 18,* 34–64.

Brady, L. (1996). Peer assistance for principals: Training, observation and feedback. *Journal of Educational Administration, 34*(2), 54–63.

Caffarella, R.S. (1993). Facilitating self-directed learning as a staff development option. *Journal of Staff Development, 14*(2), 30–34.

Caldwell, B. (2002). Scenarios for leadership and the public good in education. In K. Leithwood & P. Hallinger (Eds), *Second international handbook of educational leadership and administration* (pp. 821–848). Dordrecht: Kluwer.

Caldwell, B. (2003). Successful learning and the globalization of learning. In P. Hallinger (Ed.), *Reshaping the landscape of school leadership development: A global perspective* (pp. 23–40). Lisse, Netherlands: Swets & Zeitlinger.

Candy, P., Harri-Augstein, S., & Thomas, L. (1985). Reflection and the self-organised learner: A model of learning conversations. In D. Boud, R. Keogh, & D. Walker (Eds), *Reflection: Turning experience into learning* (pp. 100–116). New York: Kogan Page.

Cardno, C. (2003). *Action research.* Wellington: New Zealand Council for Educational Research.

Carr, W., & Kemmis, S. (1986). *Becoming critical: Education, knowledge and action research.* Lewes: Falmer.

Clandinin, D.J., & Connelly, F.M. (1995). *Teachers' professional knowledge landscapes.* New York: Teachers College Press.

Cochran-Smith, M., & Lytle, S.L. (1993). *Inside/outside: Teacher research and knowledge.* New York: Teachers College Press.

Cochran-Smith, M., & Lytle, S. (1999). Relationships of knowledge and practice: Teacher learning in communities. In A. Iran-Nejad & C.D. Pearson (Eds), *Review of research in education* (Vol. 24, pp. 251–307), Washington, DC, American Educational Research Association.

Codd, J. (1990). Managerialism: The problem with today's schools. *Delta*, *44*, 17–25.

Cohen, L., & Manion, L. (1980). *Research methods in education*. London: Croom Helm.

Collins Concise Dictionary. (1999). (4th edn). Glasgow: HarperCollins.

Costa, A.L. & Kallick, B. (1993). Through the eyes of a critical friend. *Educational Leadership*, *51*(2), 49–51.

Covey, S. (1989). *Seven habits of highly effective people*. New York: Simon & Schuster.

Covey, S.R. (1990). *Principle centred leadership*. New York: Fireside.

Dempster, N. (2001). *The professional development of school principals: A fine balance*. Professorial lecture given at Griffith University, Queensland, Australia, 24 May.

Duignan, P. (1988). Reflective management: The key to quality leadership. *International Journal of Educational Management*, *2*(2), 3–12.

Duignan, P. (1989). Reflective management: The key to quality leadership. In C. Riches & C. Morgan (Eds), *Human resource management in education* (pp. 74–90). Milton Keynes: The Open University.

Duignan, P. (2002). *The Catholic educational leader–defining authentic leadership: Veritas, caritas and gravitas*. Paper presented at International Conference: Vision and Reality, Sydney, Australian Catholic University, 4–7 August.

Duignan, P. (2004a). Forming capable leaders: From competencies to capabilities. *New Zealand Journal of Educational Leadership*, *19*(2), 5–13.

Duignan, P. (2004b) *ELIM Program*. Sydney: ACU National/Parramatta Catholic Education Office.

Dussault, M., & Barnett, B.G. (1996). Peer-assisted leadership: Reducing educational managers' professional isolation. *Journal of Educational Administration*, *34*(3), 5–14.

Earl, L., & Katz, S. (2002). Leading schools in a data-rich world. In K. Leithwood & P. Hallinger (Eds), *Second international handbook of educational leadership and administration* (pp. 1003–1024). Dordrecht: Kluwer.

Eaton, J., & Johnson, R. (2001). *Coaching successfully*. London: Dorling Kindersley.

Ebbutt, D. (1985). Educational action research: Some general concerns and specific quibbles. In R.G. Burgess (Ed.), *Issues in educational research: Qualitative methods* (pp. 152–174). London: Falmer.

Ehrich, L.C. (1996). Professional mentorship for women educators in government schools. *Journal of Educational Administration, 33*(2), 69–83.

Elbaz-Luwisch, E. (2001). Personal story as passport: Storytelling in border pedagogy. *Teaching Education, 12*(1), 81–101.

Elliott, J. (1991). Action research, practical competence and professional knowledge. In O. Zuber-Skerritt (Ed.), *Action learning for improved performance: Key contributions to the first world congress on action research and process management* (pp. 26–45). Brisbane, Qld: AEBIS.

Everard, K.B., & Morris, G. (1985). *Effective school management*. London: Paul Chapman.

Fadillah, M.I. (1997). *Professional partnership of teachers: An action research study for professional development*. Unpublished thesis, University of Waikato, Hamilton.

Foucault, M. (1977). *Discipline and punish: The birth of the prison* (A. Sheridan, Trans.). New York: Pantheon.

Freire, P. (1985). *The politics of education: Culture, power, and liberation*. South Hadley, MA: Bergin & Garvey.

Fullan, M. (1985). Change processes and strategies at the local level. *Elementary School Journal, 85*(3), 391–421.

Fullan, M. (1993). *Change forces: Probing the depths of educational reform*. London: Falmer.

Fullan, M. (2001). *Leading in a culture of change*. San Francisco, CA: Jossey-Bass.

Fullan, M. (2003a). *The moral imperative of school leadership*. Thousand Oaks, CA: Corwin.

Fullan, M. (2003b). *Change forces with a vengeance*. London: Routledge Falmer.

Fullan, M. (2005). *Leadership and sustainability: System thinkers in action.* Thousand Oaks, CA: Corwin.

Fullan, M. with Stiegelbauer, S. (1991). *The new meaning of educational change.* London: Cassell.

Gibbs, C. (2002). *Cultural efficacy: Implications for teachers and teacher education.* Paper presented at the annual conference of the New Zealand Association for Research in Education, Palmerston North, December.

Giddens, A. (1993). *New rules of sociological method* (2nd edn). Cambridge: Polity.

Giroux, H. (1992). *Border crossings: Cultural workers and the politics of education.* New York: Routledge.

Glaser, B.G., & Strauss, A.L. (1967). *The discovery of grounded theory: Strategies for qualitative research.* Chicago, IL: Aldine.

Goffman, E. (1959). *The presentation of self in everyday life.* New York: Doubleday.

Goldhammer, R. (1969). *Clinical supervision.* New York: Holt, Rinehart and Winston.

Goodlad, J.I. (1978). Educational leadership: Toward the third era. *Educational Leadership, 35*(4), 322–331.

Greene, M. (1985). The role of education in democracy. *Educational Horizons, 63* (Special issue), 3–9.

Griffin, G.A. (1987). The school in society and the social organization of the school: Implications for staff development. In M.F. Wideen & I. Andrews (Eds), *Staff development for school improvement: A focus on the teacher* (pp. 19–37). Lewes: Falmer.

Gronn, P. (2002). Leader formation. In K. Leithwood & P. Hallinger (Eds), *Second international handbook of educational leadership and administration* (pp. 1031–1070). Dordrecht: Kluwer.

Gronn, P. (2003). *The new work of educational leaders.* London: Sage.

Grossman, P., Wineburg, S., & Woolworth, S. (2000). *In pursuit of teacher community.* Paper presented at the annual meeting of the American Educational Research Association, New Orleans, April.

Grundy, S. (1993). Educational leadership as emancipatory praxis. In J. Blackmore & J. Kenway (Eds), *Gender matters in educational administration and policy* (pp. 165–177). London: Falmer.

Gunter, H. (2001). *Leaders and leadership in education.* London: Paul Chapman.

Hallinger, P. (Ed.). (2003). *Reshaping the landscape of school leadership development: A global perspective.* Lisse: Swets & Zeitlinger.

Hallinger, P., & Bridges, E. (1997). Problem-based leadership development: Preparing educational leaders for changing times. *Journal of School Leadership, 7,* 1–15.

Hallinger, P., & Murphy, J. (1985). Assessing the instructional management behavior of principals. *Elementary School Journal, 86*(2), 217–247.

Hallinger, P., & Murphy, J. (1991). Developing leaders for future schools. *Phi Delta Kappan, 72*(7), 514–520.

Halpin, D. (2003). *Hope and education: The role of the Utopian imagination.* London: Routledge Falmer.

Hargreaves, A. (2003). *Teaching in the knowledge society: Education in the age of insecurity.* New York: Teachers College Press.

Hargreaves, A. (2004). *The seven principles of sustainable leadership.* Paper presented at the 2nd International Summit for Leadership in Education, Boston, 2–6 November.

Hargreaves, A., & Fink, D. (2004). The seven principles of sustainable leadership. *Educational Leadership, 61*(7), 8–14.

Hargreaves, A., & Fullan, M. (Eds). (1992). *Teacher development and educational change.* New York: Falmer.

Hargreaves, D. (2003). *Education epidemic: Transforming secondary schools through innovation networks.* London: Demos.

Harris, A. (2004). Distributed leadership: Leading or misleading? *Educational Management and Administration, 32*(1), 11–24.

Harris, A., & Lambert, L. (2003). *Building leadership capacity for school improvement.* Maidenhead, England: Open University Press.

Hay Group. (2001). *Identifying the skills, knowledge, attributes and competencies for first-time principals: Shaping the next generation of principals.* Melbourne, Vic: Hay.

Houma, S. (1998). *A study of staff appraisal at the Solomon Islands College of Higher Education.* Unpublished M.Ed. (Leadership) thesis, University of Waikato, Hamilton.

Huber, S. (Ed.). (2003). *Preparing school leaders for the 21st century: An international comparison of development programmes in 15 countries.* London: Taylor & Francis.

Isaacs, W. (1999). *Dialogue and the art of thinking together.* New York: Doubleday.

Jasman, A.M. (2002). *Crossing borders: Learning from, by working in, different professional knowledge contexts.* Paper presented at the Conference of the Australian Association for Research in Education.

Joyce, B., & Showers, B. (1982). The coaching of teaching. *Educational Leadership, 40*(1), 4–10.

Joyce, B., & Showers, B. (1988). *Student achievement through staff development.* New York: Longman.

Kemmis, S. (1985). Action research and the politics of reflection. In D. Boud, R. Keogh, & D. Walker (Eds), *Reflection: Turning experience into learning* (pp. 139–163). New York: Kogan Page.

Kemmis, S., & McTaggart, R. (1988). *The action research planner* (3rd edn). Geelong, Vic: Deakin University.

Kolb, D.A. (1984). *Experiential learning: Experience as the source of learning and development.* Englewood Cliffs, NJ: Prentice Hall.

Lambert, L. (1998). How to build leadership capacity. *Educational Leadership, 55*(7), 17–19.

Landsberg, M. (2003). *The tao of coaching.* London: Profile.

Lange, (The Hon.) D. (1988). *Tomorrow's schools: The reform of educational administration in New Zealand.* Wellington: Government Printer.

Lee, G.V. (1991). Peer-assisted development of school leaders. *Journal of Staff Development, 12*(2), 14–18.

Lee, G.V. (1993). New images of school leadership: Implications for professional development. *Journal of Staff Development, 14*(1), 2–5.

Lee, G.V., & Barnett, B.G. (1994). Using reflective questioning to promote collaborative dialogue. *Journal of Staff Development, 15*(1), 16–21.

Lee, T. (2002). *Professional development for ICT using teachers in Hong Kong secondary schools: An action research.* Unpublished M.Ed. (Leadership) thesis, University of Waikato, Hamilton.

Leithwood, K., & Hallinger, P. (Eds). (2002). *Second international handbook of educational leadership and administration.* Dordrecht: Kluwer.

Leithwood, K., Jantzi, D., & Steinback, R. (1999). *Changing leadership for changing times.* Buckingham: Open University Press.

Lewin, K. (1948). *Resolving social conflicts: Selected papers on group dynamics.* New York: Harper & Row.

Lortie, D. (1975). *Schoolteacher.* Chicago, IL: University of Chicago Press.

Lupton, R. (2004). *Schools in disadvantaged areas: Recognising context and raising quality.* London: Economic and Social Research Council.

Marshall, T.A., & Duignan, P.A. (1987). A two-stage approach to surveying opinions. In R.J.S. Macpherson (Ed.), *Ways and meanings of research in educational administration* (University of New England Teaching Monograph No. 5, pp. 171–188). Armidale, NSW: University of New England.

Milstein, M.M., & Associates. (1993). *Changing the way we prepare educational leaders: the Danforth experience.* Newbury Park, CA: Corwin Press.

Ministry of Education. (1998). *Interim professional standards.* Wellington: Ministry of Education. Retrieved 1 February 2005 from http://www.minedu.govt.nz/

Oja, S.M., & Smulyan, L. (1989). *Collaborative action research: A developmental approach.* Lewes: Falmer.

Oliver, B. (1980). Action research for inservice training. *Educational Leadership, 37*(5), 394–395.

Popper, M., & Lipshitz, R. (1992). Coaching on leadership. *Leadership and Organization Development Journal, 13*(7), 15–18.

Robertson, J.M. (1991a). *Developing educational leadership.* Unpublished M.Ed thesis, University of Waikato, Hamilton.

Robertson, J.M. (1991b). Dilemmas faced by school principals. *The New Zealand Principal, 6*(3), 17–18.

Robertson, J.M. (1992). Statespersons, connoisseurs and entrepreneurs: The educational leaders of our schools. *The New Zealand Principal*, 7(1), 14–18.

Robertson, J.M. (1995). *Principals' partnerships: An action research study on the professional development of New Zealand school leaders.* Unpublished Ph.D thesis, University of Waikato, Hamilton.

Robertson, J.M. (1997). A programme of professional partnerships for leadership development. *Waikato Journal of Education*, 3, 137–152.

Robertson, J.M. (1999). Principals working with principals: Keeping education at the centre of practice. *set: Research Information for Teachers 1*, Item 9.

Robertson, J.M. (2000). The Three R's of action research methodology: Reciprocity, reflexivity and reflection-on-reality. *Educational Action Research*, 8(2), 307–326.

Robertson, J.M. (2004a). Leadership learning through coaching. *set: Research Information for Teachers*, 3, 44–48.

Robertson, J.M. (2004b). *Leaders coaching leaders: A workshop kit.* Hamilton: Educational Leadership Centre.

Robertson, J.M., & Allan, R. (1999). Teachers working in isolation? Creating opportunities for professional conversations. *set: Research Information for Teachers*, 2, Item 3.

Robertson, J.M., & Webber, C.F. (2000). Crosscultural leadership development. *International Journal of Leadership in Education: Theory and Practice*, 3(4), 315–330.

Robertson, J.M., & Webber, C.F. (2002). Boundary-breaking leadership: A must for tomorrow's learning communities. In K. Leithwood & P. Hallinger (Eds), *Second international handbook of educational leadership and administration* (pp. 519–553). Dordrecht: Kluwer.

Robertson, J.M., & Webber, C.F. (2004). International leadership development through web-based learning. *International Electronic Journal for Leadership in Learning*, 8(12). Available at: http://www.ucalgary.ca/~iejll/

Saphier, J., & King, M. (1986). Good seeds grow in strong cultures. *Educational Leadership*, 42(6), 67–74.

Schön, D.A. (1983). *The reflective practitioner: How professionals think in action.* New York: Basic.

Schön, D. (1987). *Educating the reflective practitioner.* San Francisco, CA: Jossey-Bass.

Senge, P. (1990). *The fifth discipline: The art and practice of the learning organization.* New York: Doubleday.

Sergiovanni, T.J. (1991). *The principalship: A reflective practice perspective* (2nd edn). Needham Heights, MA: Allyn & Bacon.

Sergiovanni, T.J. (1992). *Moral leadership: Getting to the heart of school improvement.* San Francisco, CA: Jossey-Bass.

Sergiovanni, T.J. (2001). *Leadership: What's in it for schools?* London: Routledge Falmer.

Sergiovanni, T.J. & Starratt, R.J. (1979). *Supervision: Human perspectives.* New York: McGraw-Hill.

Sergiovanni, T.J. & Starratt, R.J. (2002). *Supervision: Human perspectives* (2nd edn). New York: McGraw-Hill.

Shields, C. (2002). Focusing a crowded leadership agenda: Social justice and academic excellence. *New Zealand Journal of Educational Leadership, 17,* 33–45.

Smyth, J. (1989). A critical pedagogy of classroom practice: Educational reform at the chalkface. *Delta, 41,* 53–64.

Smyth, J. (1991). *Teachers as collaborative learners.* Buckingham: Open University Press.

Snook, I. (1990). The principal: Manager or professional leader? *The New Zealand Principal, 5*(1), 5–7.

Somekh, B. (1994). Inhabiting each other's castles: Towards knowledge and mutual growth through collaboration, *Educational Action Research, 2,* 357–382.

Southworth, G. (2002). What is important in educational administration: Learning-centred school leadership, *New Zealand Journal of Educational Leadership, 17,* 5–19.

Southworth, G., with Clunie, R., & Somerville, D. (1994). Headteacher mentoring: Insights and ideas about headteacher development. In H. Bradley, C. Connor & G. Southworth (Eds), *Developing teachers, developing schools: Making INSET effective for the school.* London: Fulton.

Starratt, R .J. (2004). *Ethical leadership.* San Francisco, CA: Jossey-Bass.

Stenhouse, L. (1975). *An introduction to curriculum research and development.* London: Heinemann.

Stewart, D. (2000). *Tomorrow's principals today.* Palmerston North: Massey University/Kanuka Grove Press.

Stewart, D., & Prebble, T. (1993). *The reflective principal: School development within a learning community.* Palmerston North: Massey University/ ERDC Press.

Stoll, L., & Bolam, R. (2005). Developing leadership for learning communities. In M. Coles & G. Southworth (Eds), *Developing leadership: Creating the schools of tomorrow* (pp. 50–64). Maidenhead: Open University Press.

Stoll, L., & Fink, D. (1996). *Changing our schools: Linking school effectiveness and school improvement.* Buckingham: Open University Press.

Strachan, J.M.B. (1999). Feminist educational leadership: Locating the concepts in practice. *Gender and Education, 11*(3), 309–322.

Strachan, J.M.B., & Robertson, J.M. (1992). Principals' professional development. *New Zealand Journal of Educational Administration, 7,* 45–51.

Strauss, A., & Corbin, J.M. (Eds). (1997). *Grounded theory in practice.* Thousand Oaks, CA: Sage.

Sutton, M. (2005). Coaching for pedagogical change, *New Zealand Journal of Educational Leadership, 20*(2), 31–46.

Thrupp, M. (2004). Conceptualising educational leadership for social justice. *New Zealand Journal of Educational Leadership, 19*(1), 21–29.

Thrupp, M., & Willmott, R. (2003). *Educational management in managerialist times: Beyond the textual apologists.* Buckingham: Open University Press.

Wadsworth, E.J. (1990). A vision of a pot of gold: School leadership and the emergence of practitioner consultants, *Delta, 44,* 49–57.

Walker, A., & Dimmock, C. (2002). Moving school leadership beyond its narrow boundaries: Developing a cross-cultural approach. In K. Leithwood & P. Hallinger (Eds), *Second international handbook of educational leadership and administration* (pp. 167–204). Dordrecht: Kluwer.

Webber, C.F., & Robertson, J. (1998). Boundary breaking: An emergent model for leadership development. *Educational Policy Analysis Archives*, 6(21). Available at: http://olam.ed.asu.edu/epaa/v6n21.html

Webber, C.F., & Robertson, J. (2004). Internationalization and educators' understanding of issues in educational leadership. *The Educational Forum*, 68(3), 264–275.

West-Burnham, J. (2004). *Building leadership capacity: Helping leaders learn. A thinkpiece for the National College for School Leaders.* Nottingham: National College for School Leaders.

Whitmore, J. (2002). *Coaching for performance: GROWing people, performance and purpose* (3rd edn). London: Nicholas Brealey.

Whyte, W.F. (Ed.). (1991). *Participatory action research.* Thousand Oaks, CA: Sage.

Wildy, H., Louden, W., & Robertson, J. (2000). Using cases for school principal performance standards: Australian and New Zealand experiences. *Waikato Journal of Education*, 6, 169–194.

Winter, R. (1989). *Learning from experience: Principles and practice in action-research.* Lewes: Falmer.

Winters, S. (1996). *Developing classroom management styles in secondary schools.* Unpublished M.Ed. thesis, University of Waikato, Hamilton.

Wylie, C. (1994). *Self-managing schools in New Zealand: The fifth year.* Wellington: New Zealand Council for Educational Research.

Wylie, C. (1997). *At the centre of the web: The role of the New Zealand primary school principal within a decentralized education system.* Wellington: New Zealand Council for Educational Research.

Zeus, P., & Skiffington, A. (2002). *The coaching at work toolkit: A complete guide to techniques and practices.* Sydney: McGraw-Hill.